Inequality:

Piketty's *Capital* in a Nutshell

Robert Schafer

ISBN-13: 978-1-7342913-0-8

Figures from Thomas Piketty's website for *Capital in the Twenty-First Century* have been used with permission.

Greenstone Press

Inequality: Piketty's *Capital* in a Nutshell

By

Robert Schafer

Thomas Piketty's *Capital in the Twenty-First Century* has made a strong impression inside and outside the economics profession. Branko Milanovic called it "one of the watershed books in economic thinking" in a review in the *Journal of Economic Literature*. Piketty describes a world in which capital (or wealth which he uses interchangeably with capital) is growing, capital is distributed very unequally, the return to capital is such that the inequality in the distribution of capital will continue to increase and as a result the inequality in the distribution of income will continually increase. Historically, he considers the developed nations on a path to return to the degree of capital dominance experienced in the 18th and 19th centuries up to World War I. He marks the beginning of this return as 1980. The period in between when the role of capital declined and the extent of income inequality declined, he attributes to the shocks of two world wars and the Great Depression. Piketty views this future in dire terms. He asks whether we can transcend capitalism or must we await the next crisis or the next war to "regulate today's global patrimonial capitalism justly as well as efficiently". (Piketty, page 471.) His solution is an annual progressive global tax on capital.

The one thing that everyone can agree on about this book is that it develops and analyzes a vast amount of data on capital, income and inequality that has not been studied before. In the case of France, Piketty's native country, the information stretches back to 1700, although the better data dates from 1790. This is also true for Britain. For others it reaches back to around 1900 for the higher quality data. The French have a history of keeping careful financial records on their citizens and this accounts for the length of time covered by the data in France. For most countries the data starts when the countries adopted an income tax. The sources of the data are probate, inheritance tax and income tax records and other similar fiscal records. All data sources are subject to limitations. These fiscal records are no exception. Fiscal records tend to include only the better off persons, that is those paying income taxes or inheritance taxes.

Since Piketty is interested in several countries, actually the whole world if the data were available, he faced the problem of comparability across countries. He solves this difficulty by constructing ratios. For example, he does not present the amount of capital in dollars or euros. Instead he measures the amount of capital in a country as the ratio of its capital to its national income. This capital/income ratio has units of "years", the number of years of national income that the country has in capital. Then these ratios can be compared across countries. A similar approach is used for nearly all the measurements presented in the book.

There is a troublesome feature in the presentation of data through figures in this book. The time scale keeps changing. This is disconcerting and often downright confusing. Sometimes the time scale runs from 1870 to 2010. Then it might run from 1700 to 2010. Other times it jumps to antiquity to 2100. It requires a conscious effort, on the part of the reader, to be on the alert as to what the time scale is on each figure. If you forget, you fall into misinterpreting the presented material. This is especially troubling for the two most important figures in the book from the perspective of Piketty's outlook on the world. These figures stretch time into the future and the past beyond the time periods for which there is data; if you are not careful you find yourself treating them as based on data even though they are clearly labelled. That's due to the fact that nearly all the figures in the book are based on data.

How does Piketty get from his data to his view of the world? The essential analytical steps of his journey are:

1. The resurgence of capital. Capital was very important at the beginning of the twentieth century, became less important in the middle of the twentieth century and has grown in importance over the past sixty years. Capital/income ratios are rising.
2. Use of a steady state economy to forecast the future. Piketty's model to forecast future values of the capital/income ratio.
3. Increasing share of income from capital. Capital's share of national income is rising in all rich countries, and this rise is

tied to the rise in the capital/income ratio through the return on capital.

4. Growing inequality in the income distribution. Changes in income inequality are assessed in relation to the roles of wages and income from capital in the incomes of the highest income persons.
5. Growing inequality in the distribution of the ownership of capital. The decrease in the concentration of the ownership of capital during the first half of the twentieth century was largely responsible for the decrease in income inequality during this period leading to a growing middle class that owned a significant share of capital. The recent trend toward increasing concentration of the ownership of capital by the top decile fuels the growing income inequality.
6. Return on capital greater than the rate of growth. For Piketty, as long as the return on capital exceeds the growth rate, the increased concentration of capital leads to increasing income inequality.
7. Role of inheritance. Inheritance exacerbates the concentration of capital and, hence, income inequality.

The following presents the essence of Piketty's presentation and provides analysis of its content. Following the discussion of these steps in Piketty's analysis is a discussion of his "fear" and his proposed solution of a tax on wealth.

Resurgence of Capital

How does Piketty define capital? "[C]apital is defined as the sum total of nonhuman assets that can be owned and exchanged on some market. Capital includes all forms of real property (including residential real estate) as well as financial and professional capital (plants, infrastructure, machinery, patents, and so on) used by firms and government agencies." (Piketty, page 46.) "It consists of the sum total of nonfinancial assets... and financial assets ... less the total amount of financial liabilities (debt)." (Piketty, page 48.)

It is important to put Piketty's definition of capital (or wealth, terms he uses interchangeably) in a context. Historically, economists used capital to refer to the means of production such as factories and machinery. This is the way capital was used by Robert Solow when he developed his model of economic growth. However, Solow soon discovered that physical capital alone could not explain the development of the United States in the twentieth century. This led eventually to the introduction of another capital concept: human capital. Human capital is the acquired knowledge and skills, whether through formal education or informally, by human beings. More recently, a third type of capital has been recognized: social capital which refers to the networks that connect people, groups and firms and facilitate cooperation within or among groups increasing trust between participants. Neither human capital nor social capital is included in Piketty's definition of capital. Some have objected to Piketty's exclusion of human capital because they view wages as compensation partly for the raw labor that workers supply and partly for the skills acquired through education and training, the latter being human capital. But this division has probably been possible throughout the period Piketty studied, and it is hard to justify treating it differently over time due to difficulties in measuring human capital. Even though the concept of human capital is helpful for some purposes, it seems appropriate to treat all wages as labor compensation if one is interested in the shares of national income going to labor and capital as Piketty is. Social capital involves externalities at every turn, it being the interrelationships among participants that is its essence. Measuring the value of social capital in a capital context is fraught with difficulties and probably impossible over the time period that Piketty studies.

How does Piketty measure the importance of capital in a country? He calculates the ratio of capital to national income. A major benefit of this is that it means that the differences in currencies and exchange rates can be dispensed with when comparing across countries, and the changes in price can be ignored when comparing a country across time. This leads us to the definition of national income. Piketty defines national income "as the sum of all income available to the residents of a given country in a given year, regardless of the legal classification of that income." (Piketty, page 43.) National income is equal to gross domestic product minus the depreciation of the capital that made this production possible and minus net income from abroad. National income excludes all taxes and monetary transfers. (Piketty, page 180.) Capital is a stock and national income is a flow.

Piketty shows that capital was very dominant before the first World War being as high as seven times national income in some European countries, became less important during the next 40 years declining to about three times national income and has been growing in importance over the last 60 years (his data ends in 2010). Figure 4.5 is reproduced from the technical appendix to his book (all figures from Piketty's book are reproduced from that appendix and are the same as those appearing in the printed copy.) Figure 4.5 shows the national capital/income ratio for three countries (Germany, France and the United Kingdom) for the period from 1870 to 2010. The national capital/income ratio in all three countries was around 700% from 1870 to 1910. Piketty has data for France and the United Kingdom that shows that the national capital/income ratio was at this level back to 1700. This means that during those years capital was equal to 7 times the national income. (Piketty uses percentages instead of the ratio; either convey the same information.) Starting in 1910 in all three countries the national capital income ratio declines, quite precipitously, to 3 to 3.5 times national income in 1920 and then to 2.5 to 3 times national income in 1950. Then the national capital/income ratio climbs to 3 to 3.5 times national income in 1970 in all three countries. The three countries' paths diverge over the rest of the period. The United Kingdom begins growing before the other two and grows to slightly over 5 times national income in 2010. France and Germany remain at around 3.5 times national income until 1990. Then France grows quite rapidly to a national capital/income ratio of 6 in

2010, and Germany grows more slowly to a national capital/income ratio of slightly over 4 in 2010.

What happened in the United States? Figure 4.8 from Piketty's book shows the national capital/national income ratio for the United States as well as the private capital/national income ratio and the public capital/national income ratio for 1770 to 2010. These two figures have different time scales and, therefore, have to be read accordingly. The period between 1870 and 2010 in Figure 4.8 needs to be compared with Figure 4.5. It is very different from what the three European countries experienced. In the United States, the national capital/income ratio never reached the heights that it rose to in Germany, France and the United Kingdom; the United States' ratio is generally below 5 with the exception of 1930. In addition, the portion of the graph covering 1770 to 1870 had national capital/income ratios around 300 percent, less than half the values Piketty reports for the three European countries during those time periods. Furthermore, although the national capital/income ratio grew from 1950 to 2010, it only increased from just under 4 to just over 4. This change was nothing like the increase in the three European countries.

Piketty has to explain why the national capital/income ratio dropped dramatically after 1910 and why the United States' experience is so different. The drop came about, he explains, because of the shocks of two World Wars and the Great Depression. These events destroyed much of the existing capital and also enabled the adoption of high graduated

Figure 4.5. National capital in Europe, 1870-2010

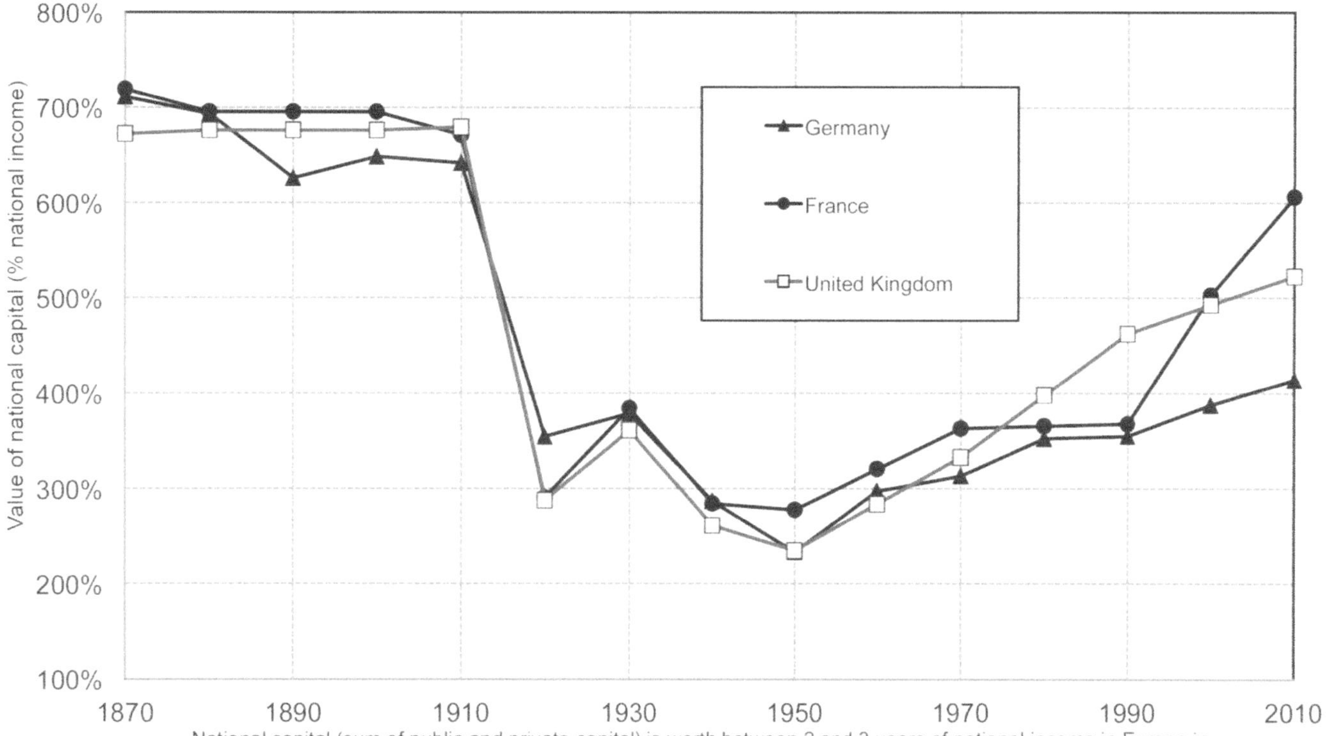

National capital (sum of public and private capital) is worth between 2 and 3 years of national income in Europe in 1950. Sources and series: see piketty.pse.ens.fr/capital21c

Figure 4.8. Private and public capital in the U.S., 1770-2010

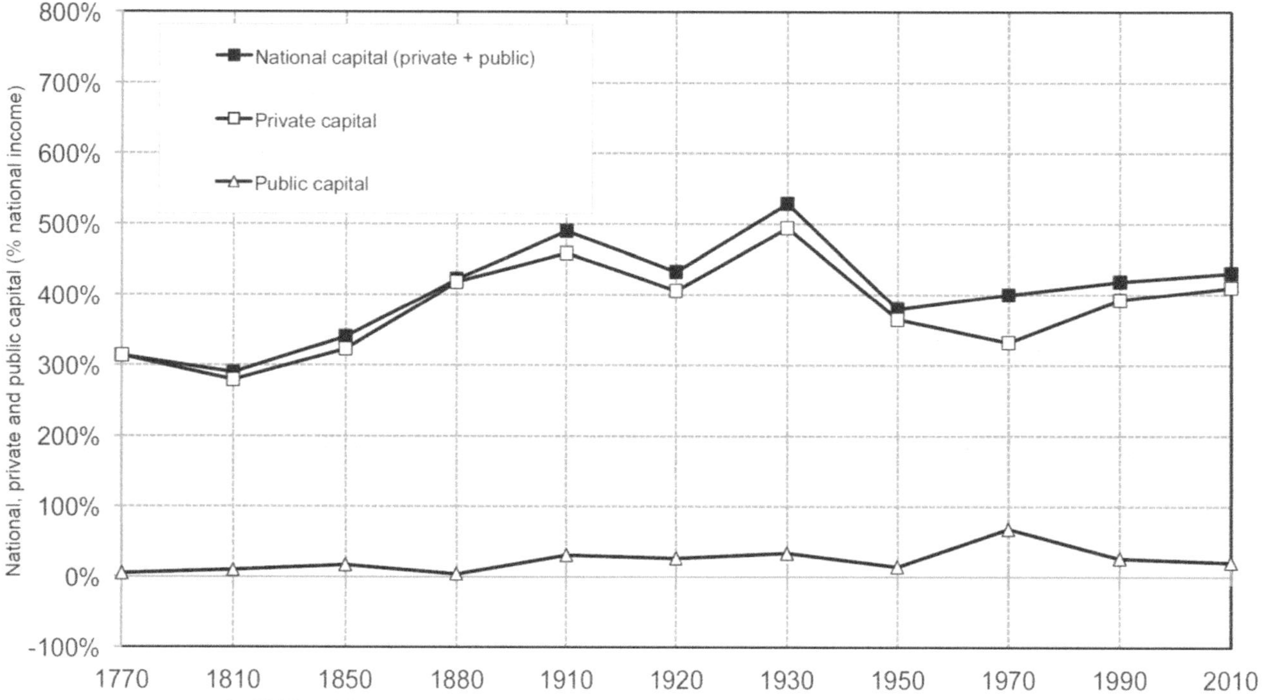

In 2010, public capital is worth 20% of national income, vs. over 400% for private capital.
Sources and series: see piketty.pse.ens.fr/capital21c

taxes and the expenditure of large social welfare programs (such as social security in the United States).

Piketty wants to present a case that the national capital/income ratio has a u-shape between 1910 and 2010 as a basic underpinning of his analysis. The European experience fits into this scenario very neatly, but the United States' experience does not. Piketty ascribes the low levels of the national capital/income ratios in the United States before 1890 to the abundant supply of land relative to that in Europe and the accompanying very low price of land in the United States plus the low level of other forms of capital due to it being a new world without much accumulated capital and also the role of slavery in the southern states. This, however, does not help him with his desired u-shaped curve for the twentieth century. Here he is left with pointing out that the United States was less affected by the shocks and that the u-shaped curve is "smaller in amplitude". The shape is formed by a decline from 1930 to 1950 from a national capital/income ratio of just over 5 to one just under 4. But why was the United States' ratio higher in 1930 than it was in 1910?

One question is whether the measure of national income is an underestimate in the earlier periods, especially in the eighteenth and early nineteenth centuries, because of the role of non-cash payments in the economy such as on-site consumption of agricultural products and payments in kind through goods or services (i.e., a larger barter economy). In 1700, roughly 60 percent of the capital in Britain and France was agricultural land. (Piketty, pages 116-117.) If the national income attributable to the agricultural land is undercounted, the capital/national income ratio is over estimated. It could well be significantly lower in the 1700s and 1800s than the numbers Piketty uses.

The Future for Capital/Income Ratios

Since Piketty wants to discuss the future in terms of what is going to happen to the capital/income ratios, his challenge is to find a way to forecast the future values of the capital/income ratios. He does this through what he calls the Second Fundamental Law of Capitalism. In his words, "[i]n the long run, the capital/income ratio β is related in a simple and transparent way to the savings rate s and the growth rate g according to the following formula $\beta=s/g$". (Piketty, page 166.) He goes on to state that his Second Fundamental Law of Capitalism "is applicable only if certain crucial assumptions are satisfied. First, this is an asymptotic law, meaning that it is only valid in the long run....Second, the law ... is valid only if one focuses on those forms of capital that human beings can accumulate.... Finally, the law ... is valid only if asset prices evolve on average in the same way as consumer prices." (Piketty, pages 168-69.)

To understand Piketty's Second Law, it is necessary to understand where it comes from. In his technical appendix, Piketty explains that he arrives at his Second Law from the relationship between capital this year and capital last year. More specifically, the amount of capital this year is equal to the amount of capital last year plus the amount of income saved last year, net of capital depreciation. Notice that these are amounts and not ratios. They are converted to ratios by dividing by this year's income. That makes the left-hand side of the equation equal to this year's capital/income ratio. The other side is more complicated because it is necessary to replace this year's income on the right side with its relationship to last year's income. This year's income equals last year's income plus the growth rate times last year's income. (The growth rate is the rate by which last year's income grew (or declined) to this year's income.) After mathematical substitution and rearrangement, a relationship results. (See the Appendix for the details on these calculations.)

The resulting relationship is not Piketty's Second Fundamental Law. Instead, it is a relationship that describes the behavior of the capital/income ratio from last year to this year as depending on last year's savings rate and last year's growth rate. More specifically, there are different possibilities:

1. This year's capital/income ratio will be <u>greater than</u> last year's if last year's savings rate is <u>greater than</u> the product of last year's capital/income ratio and last year's growth rate.
2. This year's capital/income ratio will be <u>equal to</u> last year's if last year's savings rate is <u>equal to</u> the product of last year's capital/income ratio and last year's growth rate.
3. This year's capital/income ratio will be <u>less than</u> last year's if last year's savings rate is <u>less than</u> the product of last year's capital/income ratio and last year's growth rate.

Only one of these leads to Piketty's Second Law, the middle one. This presents the question of which, if any, of these three circumstances will reflect the long run. Here is the reason that Piketty emphasizes that his Second Law is asymptotic and only applicable in the long run. But he never actually takes any steps to show that the relationship from which he plucks his Second Law is asymptotic. Even more strangely for a book whose hallmark is data, he does not explore whether his data support his claim of asymptotic behavior.

What is an asymptote? An asymptote is a line that a curve approaches as the variable approaches plus or minus infinity. The essence of an asymptote is that it is a limit on a function as the variable(s) of interest approach plus or minus infinity. The relationship that Piketty claims to be asymptotic is not asymptotic. It is a function of last year's savings rate, last year's growth rate and last year's capital/income ratio; these are the three possible variables that could lead to an asymptotic result. It makes no sense to examine the result when last year's savings rate and/or last year's growth rate approach infinity because these rates are generally much less than one. Even if one did do this, there would be no asymptotic result. Similarly, it makes no sense to look at the result of letting last year's capital/income ratio approach infinity as that would result in this year's capital/income ratio approaching infinity, a result devoid of meaning. There is one more possibility; that the time variable be looked at as approaching infinity. This results in a complex expression that does not behave asymptotically. Piketty's underlying relationship does not show any asymptotic behavior.

It is interesting that in a later article with Gabriel Zucman, the authors do not refer to Piketty's Second Fundamental Law of Capitalism, but instead they appeal to the Harrod-Domar-Solow model to support the same relationship contained in Piketty's Second Law. That model produces that formula under certain assumptions in the long run for a steady state solution. The problem with this approach is that the steady state solution to the Solow growth model begs the question of whether such a solution is an asymptotic result for the model. The steady state Solow model assumes that the savings rate and the growth rate are constant; this is what makes it a steady state situation. It permits various insights. It is not a foundation for what Piketty is trying to do, forecast the future capital/income ratio. The Solow model has additional assumptions that have the capital approaching the long run value from below at a decreasing rate. It is interesting that Piketty relies on the Solow model which is a mathematical model given that he holds some disdain for them; Piketty describes them as being "frequently no more than an excuse for occupying the terrain and masking the vacuity of the content". (Piketty, page 574.)

The derivation of the relationship underlying Piketty's Second Law suggests some empirical analysis. For example, the relationship suggests what should happen to this year's capital/income ratio relative to last year's capital/income ratio. Piketty has the data to graph this year's capital/income ratio minus last year's capital/income ratio against time. He also has the data to graph last year's savings rate minus the product of last year's capital/income ratio times last year's growth rate against time. Figure 1 is this graph for the United States from 1917 to 2010 for national capital/income ratios. (A plot of these curves for the private capital/income ratio for the United States over the same period looks similar to Figure 1.) The two terms move fairly closely in parallel for the period except for the years 1995-2010. The correlation coefficient for the 1917-2010 period is 0.37. If the correlation coefficient is calculated for the period 1917-1994, it rises to 0.42. What has happened in the 1995-2010 period? One reason for the deviations between these two terms could be the violation of Piketty's assumption that asset and consumer prices evolve on average in the same way. If they do not, capital gains and losses need to be taken into account. When this is done, there is still no asymptotic relationship. (See the Appendix for details.)

Piketty's data cover a significant period of time. What constitutes the long run? He presents summary data on the savings rate and the growth rate for a 40-year period of 1970-2010 leaving the implication that forty years is a long enough period of time. His forecasts show that he is only interested through 2100. Piketty has the data that allows one to calculate a forty year moving average for the savings rate and for the growth rate. A forty year moving average is the average of the rates over

Figure 1. Change in National Capital/Income Ratio (β_t - β_{t-1}) Compared With Changes in s_{t-1} - $\beta_{t-1}g_{t-1}$: United States 1917-2012

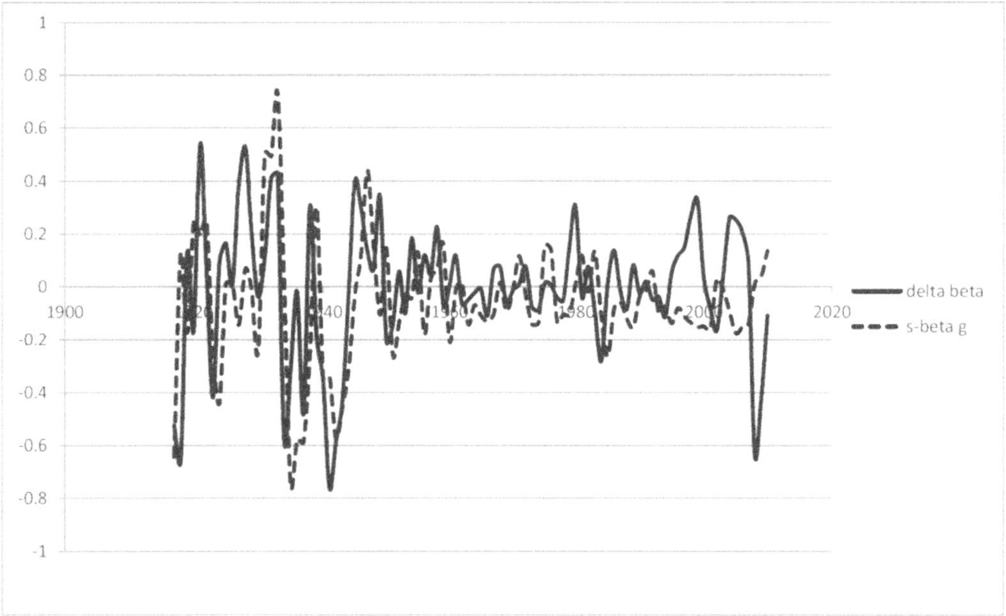

Source: Based on data in the Zucman-Piketty usa,xls file, Table US.5b

a forty year period but each year the oldest year drops out and the next one at the end of the forty year period is added in. These have been calculated for the United States for 1891 to 1990. The forty year moving average of the savings rate divided by the forty year moving average of the growth rate can be viewed as a long run estimate of the capital/income ratio using Piketty's Second Law. The observed national capital/income ratios and the so-called long run estimates of the national capital/income ratios are plotted in Figure 2. The observed national capital/income ratio does not behave as if it is approaching the long run national capital/income ratio. Instead it always lies above the long run capital/income ratio. This is contrary to the prediction of the Solow model which has the capital component approaching the long run value from below. In addition, in recent times the long run capital/income ratio is falling and not rising as Piketty claims.

Piketty highlighted the private savings rate in his Table 5.1. Does this mean that he is more interested in the private capital/income ratio? When Figure 2 is reproduced for private capital/income ratios, the results are similar, but the two lines are closer to each other and the observed and long run private capital/income ratios are moving in the same direction during the most recent twenty years; both are increasing.

Figure 2. Observed and Long Run Beta for National Capital: 1891-1990

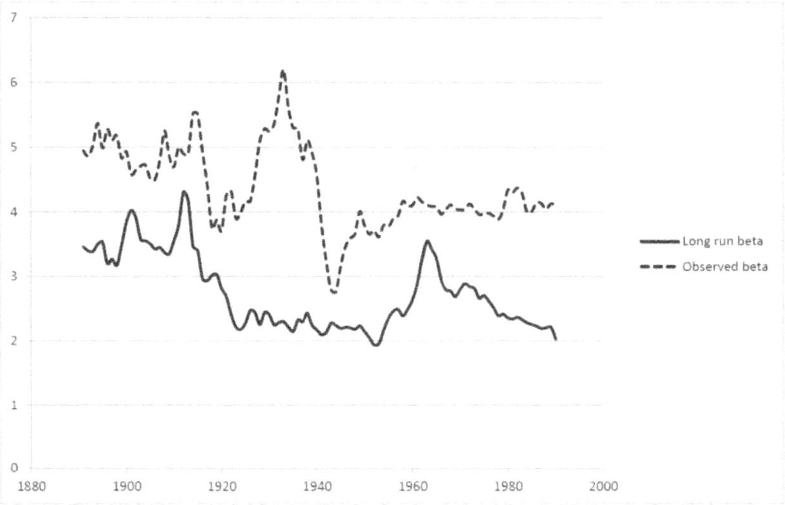

Source: Zucman-Piketty usa.xls file, Table US.5b.

What does Piketty do with his Second Fundamental Law? He uses it to project into the future. He does this by making assumptions that the global growth rate will decline to 1.5 percent annually and the savings rate will stabilize at 10 percent annually in the second half of the twenty-first century; these assumptions are fed into his Second Law with the result of a projected capital/income ratio of just under 7, which he generalizes to 7. However, he desires a graph of global capital/income ratios, but his data is limited to a few countries with a long time span. He has data on Japan back to 1905. For the period 1970-2010, he increases the countries covered to include Australia, Britain, Canada, France, Germany, Italy, Japan and the United States. But for Asia, Africa and South America, he only has data for the period after 1990. For these areas, he assumes that their earlier behavior was similar to their post 1990 behavior on average. In light of his concern with the shocks of war, this seems like a curious assumption for Asia where China was decimated by World War II and its following civil war. In any case, he combines these ideas to arrive at Figure 5.8 which purports to cover 1870 to 2100.

The thing to remember about this Figure is that the time axis has changed and that this figure is a Eurocentric view of the world as it is largely based on data from the developed world. Everything after 2010 is little more than speculation, especially given the lack of support for his Second Law.

Figure 5.8. The world capital/income ratio, 1870-2100

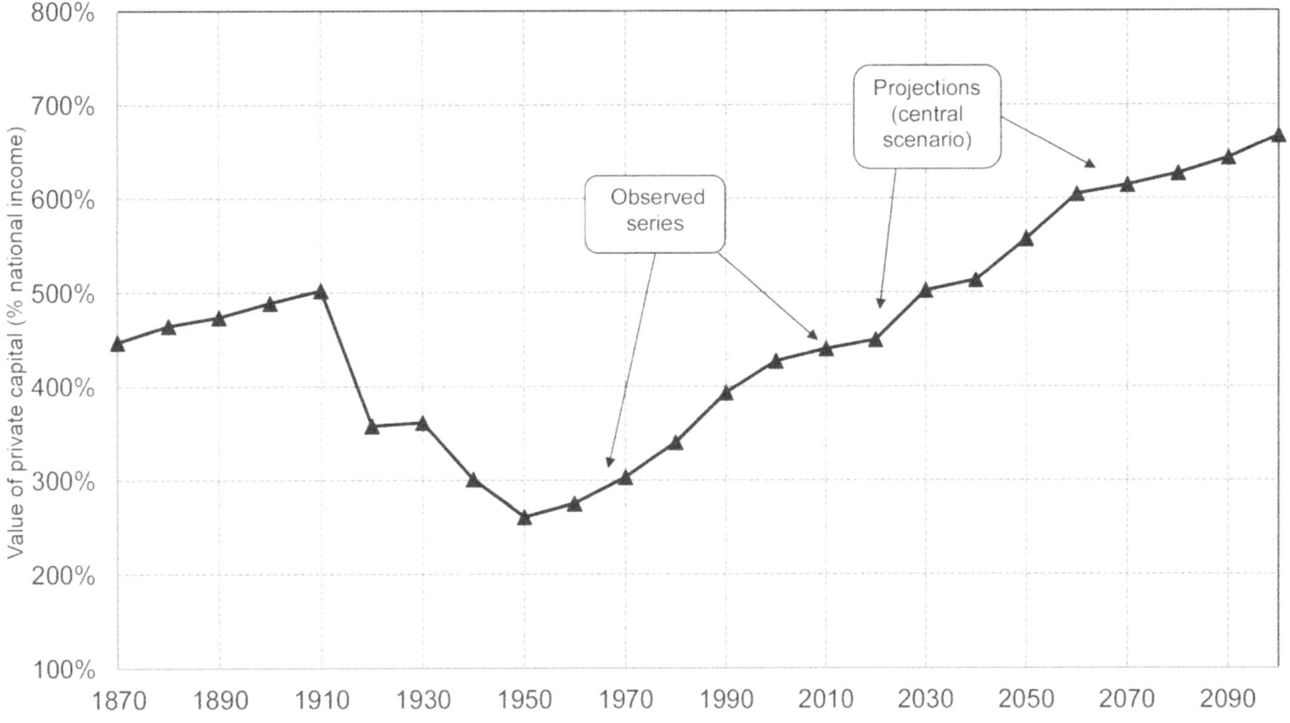

According to simulations (central scenario), the world capital/income ratio could be near to 700% by the end of the 21st century. Sources and series: see piketty.pse.ens.fr/capital21c.

Capital's Share of Income

After presenting information on the capital/income ratio, Piketty examines capital's share of national income. His Figure 6.8 shows the shares of national income going to capital for France from 1900 to 2010. Capital's share during this period peaked in 1913 and 1924-28 at around 40 percent and went as low as about 5 percent at the end of World War II. Since 1950, it has been between 20 and 30 percent except for dropping below 20 percent between 1976 and 1986 bottoming out at about 15 percent in 1983. A graph covering a longer time period (1820-2010) but with only decennial averages shows a peak at 40 percent of national income in 1850-60. A similar decennial graph for Britain for the period 1770 to 2010 shows capital's share of national income also peaking in 1850-60 but reaching a low point of 20 percent in 1920 and 1970; since 1910, it has fluctuated in Britain between 20 and 30 percent.

Figure 6.8. The capital share in national income in France, 1900-2010

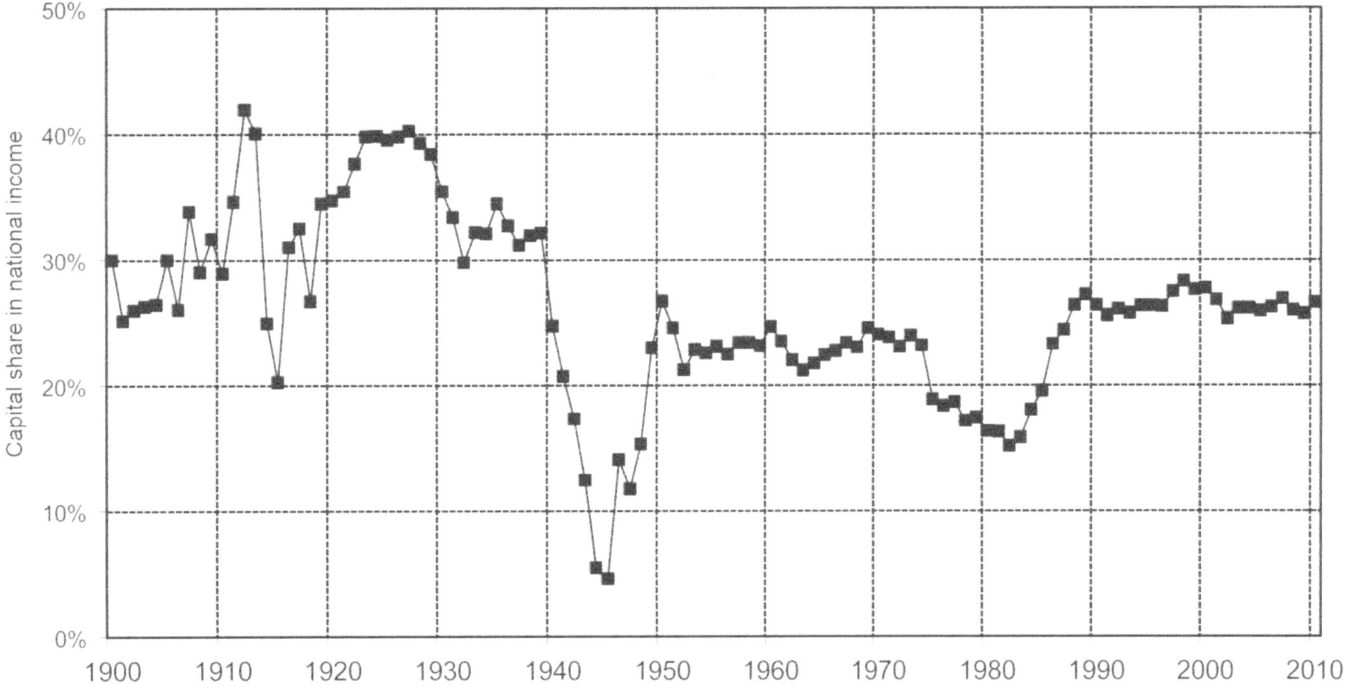

The share of capital income (net profits and rents) rose from 15% of national income in 1982 to 27% in 2010. Sources and series: see piketty.pse.ens.fr/capital21c.

Piketty expands the countries examined for the period after 1975. Figure 6.5 shows these results for capital's share of national income in Australia, Britain, Canada, France, Germany, Italy, Japan and the United States. This figure shows a considerable variation in capital's share of national income, particularly during 1975-1985. Italy has the highest capital share of national income for nearly this entire period of 1975-2010. The United States is steadily between 20 and 25 percent of national income from 1975 to 1995 and then it rises above 25 percent in 1996, 1997, 2005-2007 and 2010, with a peak at close to 30 percent in 2010. For the most part, capital's share of national income since 1995 has been between 20 and 30 percent, the exceptions being Italy and, more recently, Germany. What does Piketty conclude from his Figure 6.5? He states that "the available data indicate that capital's share of [national] income increased in most rich countries between 1970 and 2010". (Piketty, page 221.)

Capital's share of national income is related to the capital/income ratio through the return on capital *r*. The product of the return on capital and the capital/income ratio is equal to capital's share of national income. This is just an accounting definition. But Piketty calls this identity his First Fundamental Law of Capitalism. This relationship will prove useful to Piketty when he projects his capital/income ratio into the future as a means of looking at the income from capital.

Figure 6.5. The capital share in rich countries, 1975-2010

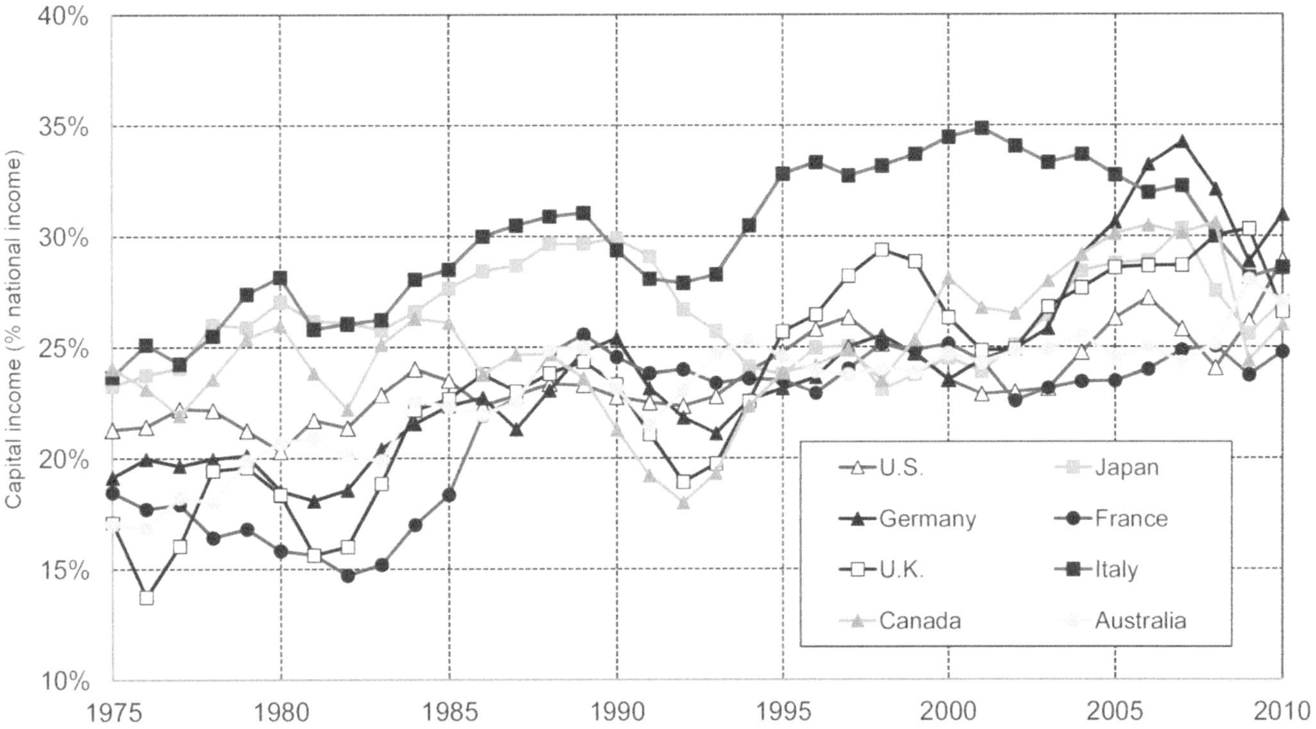

Capital income absorbs between 15% and 25% of national income in rich countries in 1970, and between 25% and 30% in 2000-2010. Sources and series: see piketty.pse.ens.fr/capital21c

Growing Inequality in the Income Distribution

Piketty examines the distribution of income by studying the share of income received by various centiles or deciles of the income distribution. For example, he answers questions like how much of the total income goes to the top ten percent of the income distribution (i.e., the top decile). Total income is "the sum of income from labor and income from capital". (Piketty, page 246,) Total income is another name for national income. Since he is French and also based in France, he starts with that country. His Figures 8.1 and 8.2 show the share of total income (one line in each graph) and of total wages (the other line in each graph) that are received by the top decile and the top centile or percentile (i.e., the top one percent) for France between 1910 and 2010. (The people in a decile or centile are changing over time; some drop out and some others join.)

Figure 8.1 shows that in France the share of total income received by the top decile declined sharply from the mid 1930s to the mid 1940s. Prior to the mid 1930s, the top decile (10 percent) received 40-47 percent of total income and after 1950, it received 30-35 percent except for a brief period of slightly over 35 percent in the 1960s. For the past twenty years, the share of the top decile has been fairly steady at around 33 percent of total income. The story for total wages is quite different; the top decile's share of total wages has generally been just over 25 percent except for the two World Wars when it fell below 25 percent. This implies that the role

Figure 8.1. Income inequality in France, 1910-2010

Inequality of total income (labor and capital) has dropped in France during the 20th century, while wage inequality has remained the same. Sources and series: see piketty.pse.ens.fr/capital21c.

Figure 8.2. The fall of rentiers in France, 1910-2010

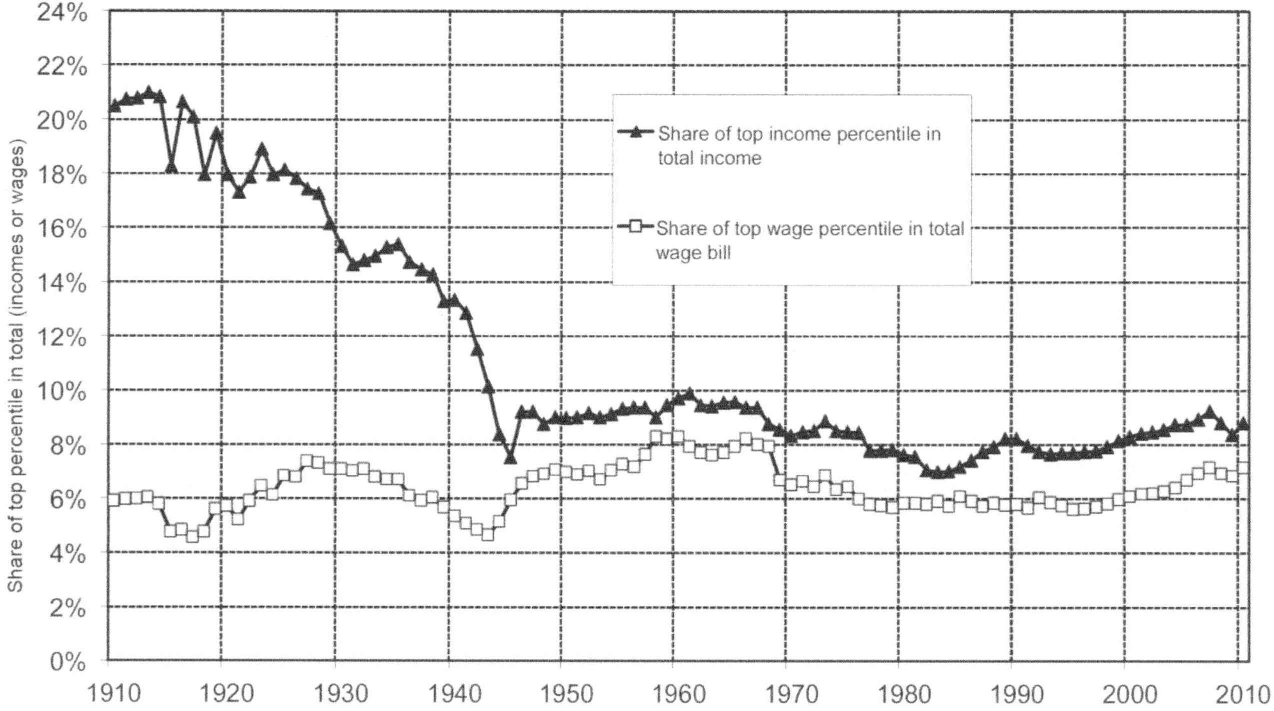

The fall in the top percentile share (the top 1% highest incomes) in France between 1914 and 1945 is due to the fall of top capital incomes. Sources and series: see piketty.pse.ens.fr/capital21c.

of wages in the share of total income received by the top decile increased over time and the role of income from capital declined over time.

The relative role of wages and income from capital in the total income of the top decile discussed above is only an implication because the top decile in total income is not identical to the top decile in total wages, although there may be a considerable overlap. For this reason, Piketty presents the source of income for the component parts of the top decile in two different years, 1932 and 2005. These are shown in his Figures 8.3 and 8.4 (not reproduced here). The horizontal axis in these two figures are intervals in the percentiles within the top decile. For example, P90-95 includes those persons between the ninetieth and ninety-fifth percentile. Both figures show that the role of income from labor declines as the income rises which is no surprise for the top decile. "There is one striking difference, however: today one has to climb much higher in the social hierarchy before income from capital outweighs income from labor. Currently, income from capital exceeds income from labor only in the top 0.1 percent of the income distribution." (Piketty. Page 277.) As Piketty points out, the source of the data in Figures 8.3 and 8.4 is income tax returns and, due to tax havens that permit capital to be hidden from tax authorities and certain exemptions, the income from capital is probably understated.

Figure 8.2 repeats the analysis of Figure 8.1 but focuses on the top centile or percentile. It shows that the top centile experienced the same trends as the top decile, but that the role of income from capital in the share of total income received by the top centile declined even more than it did for the top decile. Piketty describes the top centile in the prewar period as rentiers, namely persons and families living off of accumulated capital. He refers to the declining role of income from capital after World War I as "the fall of rentiers in France". (Piketty, page 273.)

The next country for which Piketty presents income distribution information is the United States. Piketty's Figure 8.5 shows the top decile's share of national income in the United States from 1910 to 2010. Comparing this figure to the equivalent one for France, Figure 8.1, reveals that the behavior of these two countries is very different. Whereas the United States' top decile's share of national income starts out at around 40 percent in 1910, France's started out at around 45 percent. More striking is the pattern after 1980; the top decile's share of national income in the United States grew from around 32 percent to over 45 percent reaching nearly 50 percent in 2007 while France's remained below 35 percent. Both countries show large declines during World War II. Inequality has increased substantially in the United States starting around 1980 but not in France. The top decile's share of national income in the United States is also more volatile than in France. The other line in

Figure 8.5. Income inequality in the United States, 1910-2010

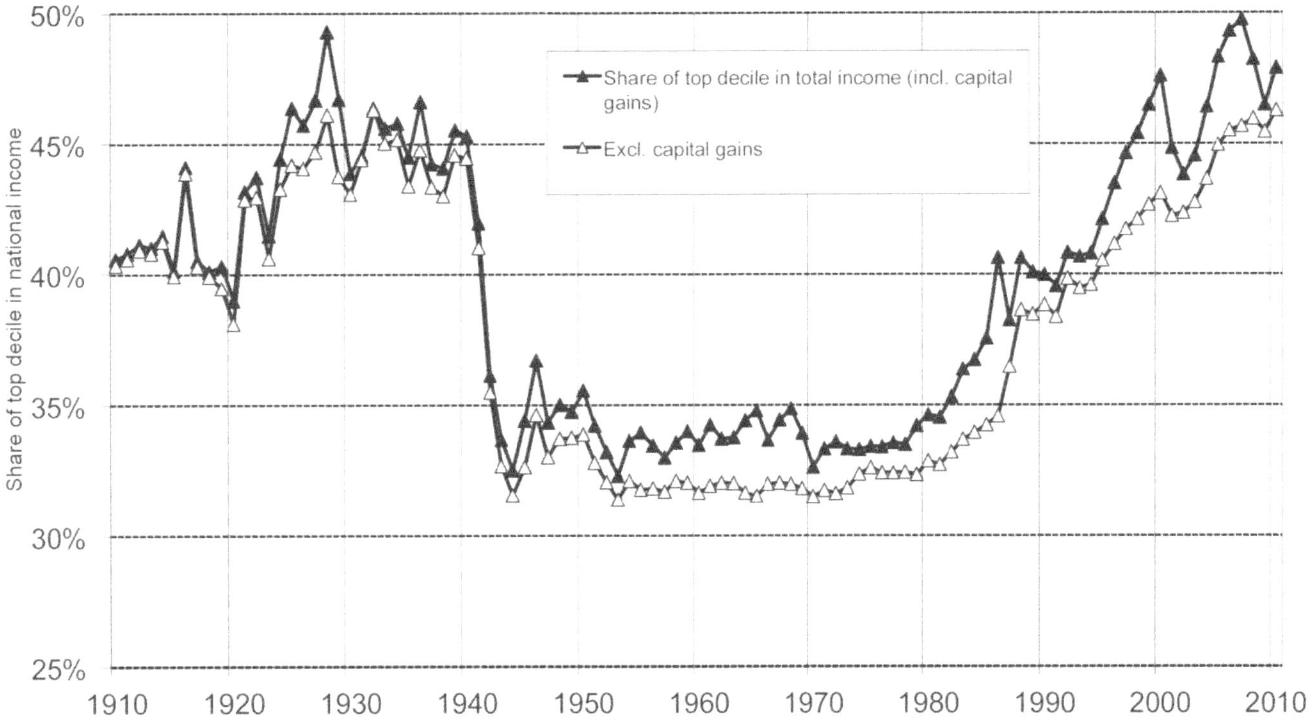

The top decile income share rose from less than 35% of total income in the 1970s to almost 50% in the 2000s-2010s.
Sources and series: see piketty.pse.ens.fr/capital21c.

Figure 8.5 graphs the top decile's share without capital gains. (information on capital gain income is generally under reported due to tax havens and tax regulations.) By excluding capital gains, two things become apparent: the volatility declines and the extent of the increase in the top decile's share is not dependent on capital gains. The large peaks in the top decile's share of United States' national income (including capital gains) in 2001 and 2007 are due to the internet bubble and the housing bubble, respectively. Without capital gains, the top decile's share increases by fourteen percentage points after 1980 in the United States, a very large increase in inequality.

Figure 8.6 shows the shares of national income received by three segments of the top decile, namely, the top centile, the top 1-5 percent group and the top 5-10 percent group. This figure shows that the bulk of the increase in inequality has gone to benefit the top centile; the top centile's share of national income has risen from around 10 percent in 1980 to about 20 percent in the 2000s. At the same time the share received by the top 1-5 percent increased from around 13 percent in 1980 to 16 percent in 2010; and the share received by the top 5-10 percent barely increased. The increasing inequality in the United States has benefited the richest of the rich the most.

What role did wages play in the changing inequality in the United States? Piketty's Figure 8.7 repeats the information contained in his Figure 8.5 and adds the graph of the top deciles of wages. The top decile's

Figure 8.6. Decomposition of the top decile, U.S. 1910-2010

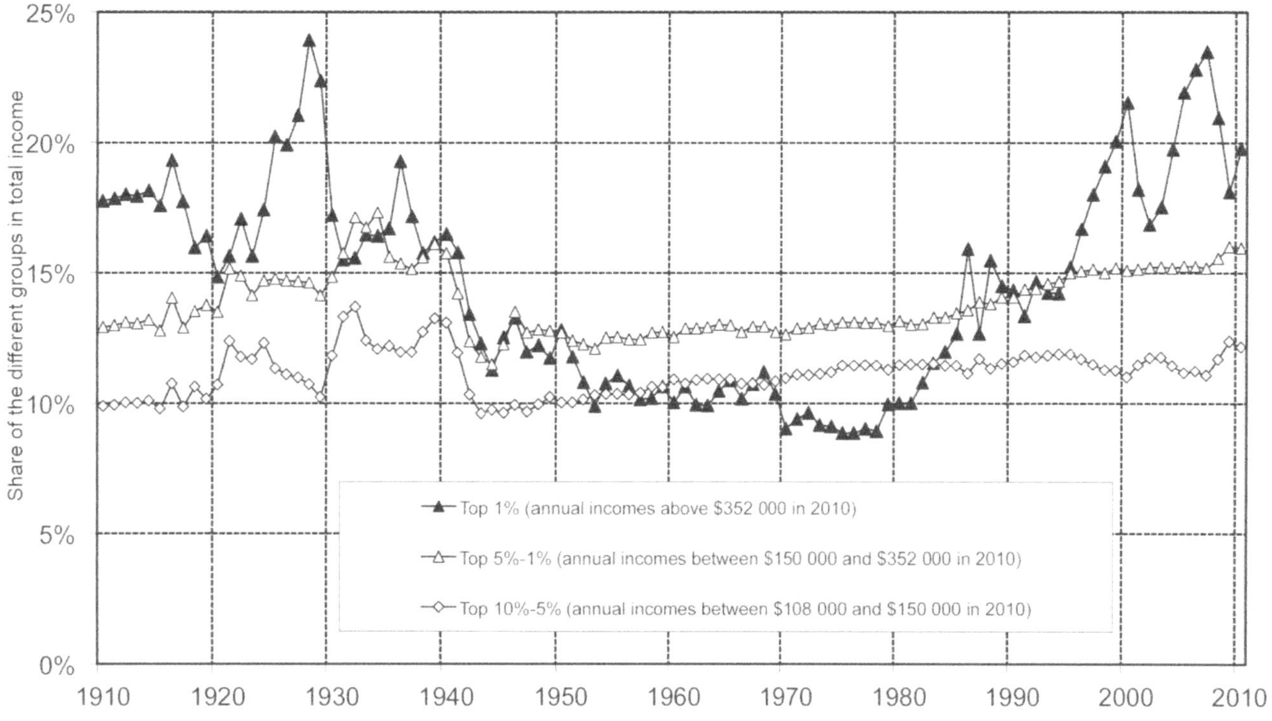

The rise of the top decile income share since the 1970s is mostly due to the top percentile.
Sources and series: see piketty.pse.ens.fr/capital21c.

Figure 8.7. High incomes and high wages in the U.S. 1910-2010

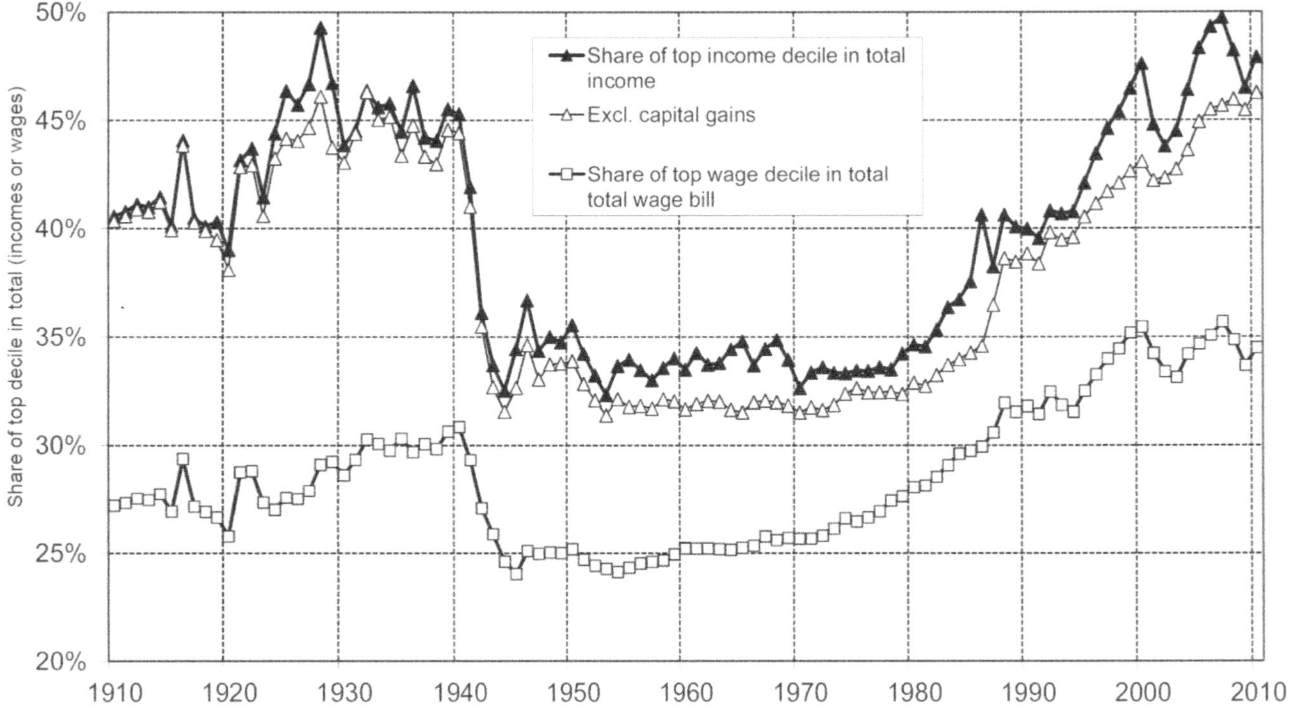

The rise of income inequality since the 1970s is largely due to the rise of wage inequality.
Sources and series: see piketty.pse.ens.fr/capital21c.

share of wages is quite different than what was observed for France. While France's top decile's share of wages was fairly stable at just over 25 percent, the United States' top decile's share of wages rose from about 25 percent in 1970 to around 35 percent in the 2000s, an increase of 10 percentage points and an increase of 40 percent over the 1970 level. Figure 8.8 shows the same information contained in Figure 8.7 except it is limited to the top centile; it shows that the top centile's share of wages rose from 5 percent in 1970 to around 22 percent in the 2000s, an even more dramatic increase than that experienced by the top decile as a group.

The implication from Figures 8.7 and 8.8 is that wage inequality is playing a major role in the Unites States' increasing income inequality. Remember that the persons in the top decile of income are not identical with those in the top decile of wages, although they probably overlap extensively. The same was true in the discussion of France. As in the case of France, Piketty calculates two graphs of the shares of United States' income coming from capital, labor and mixed sources for two years, 1929 and 2007, for the component parts of the top decile of the income distribution. As in the case of France, these show (a) an increasing role of income from capital and a decreasing role of income from labor as one moves higher in in the income distribution in both years, and (b) a more important role for labor in 2007 than in 1929 with labor income outweighing capital income until the top 0.1 percent.

Figure 8.8. The transformation of the top 1% in the United States

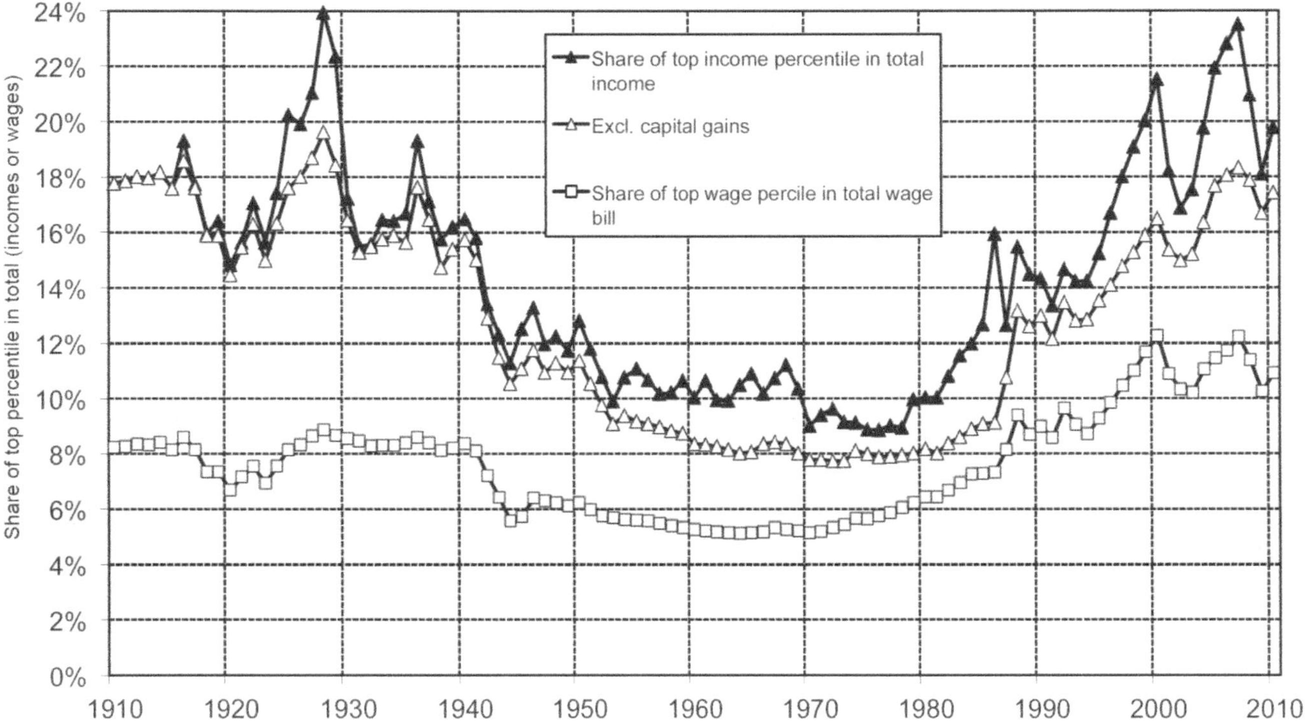

The rise in the top 1% highest incomes since the 1970s is largely due to the rise in the top 1% highest wages. Sources and series: see piketty.pse.ens.fr/capital21c.

A major difference between France and the United States is the role of wages in the growing inequality in the United States. Piketty attributes much of this increase in wage inequality to a group he refers to as “supermanagers”. These are “top executives of large firms who have managed to obtain extremely high, historically unprecedented compensation packages for their labor”. (Piketty, page 302.) This group first emerged in the United States. Piketty argues that the best explanation of the rise of the supermanagers is the change in the highest marginal income tax rates in the United States. The highest United States’ marginal income tax rate was around 90 percent in the 1950s dropping to 70 percent for the period 1966-1982. Then the highest marginal income tax rate in the United States fell to 40 percent or less in some years. Piketty argues that before the highest marginal tax rates declined, executives had little reason to bargain for large compensation packages because most of the extra compensation would be paid to the government. But when the rates were lowered, these executives had good reason to seek large compensation packages as they would now retain over half of them. He argues persuasively that the size of these supermanager compensation packages cannot be explained by the managers human capital or by their contributions to productivity. (Piketty, pages 508-512.) The experience in Britain paralleled that in the United States, while other European countries, that did not substantially lower their highest marginal tax rates, did not experience the same supermanager compensation growth. Note that the highest marginal income tax rate in France remained near 60 percent until around 2007.

Piketty draws a contrast between income inequality in Anglo-Saxon countries and other developed countries. His Figures 9.2 and 9.3 illustrate this. Figure 9.2 shows the top centile's share of income in Australia, Canada, the United Kingdom and the United States from 1910 to 2010. Figure 9.3 shows the top centile's share of income in France, Germany, Japan and Sweden from 1910 to 2010. As in all these curves, there is a considerable amount of country to country variation. However, the general trend since the 1980s in the Anglo-Saxon countries is increasing inequality (the share of the top centile is increasing significantly except for Australia). On the other hand, the share of the top centile in continental Europe and Japan shows only a slight increase. In explaining this difference, Piketty points to the role of the supermanagers in the Anglo-Saxon countries as driving income inequality there, but playing a far smaller role in continental Europe and Japan. He attributes this to differences in social norms.

What does Piketty have to report about emerging countries? His Figure 9.9 shows the top centiles share of income in Argentina, China, Colombia, India, Indonesia and South Africa from the first part of the twentieth century to 2010 (except the data for Colombia is limited to the last fifteen or so years of the period). In general, these emerging countries exhibit rising income inequality over the last twenty years (except in the case of Colombia). It would have been interesting to also see these results

Figure 9.2. Income inequality in Anglo-saxon countries, 1910-2010

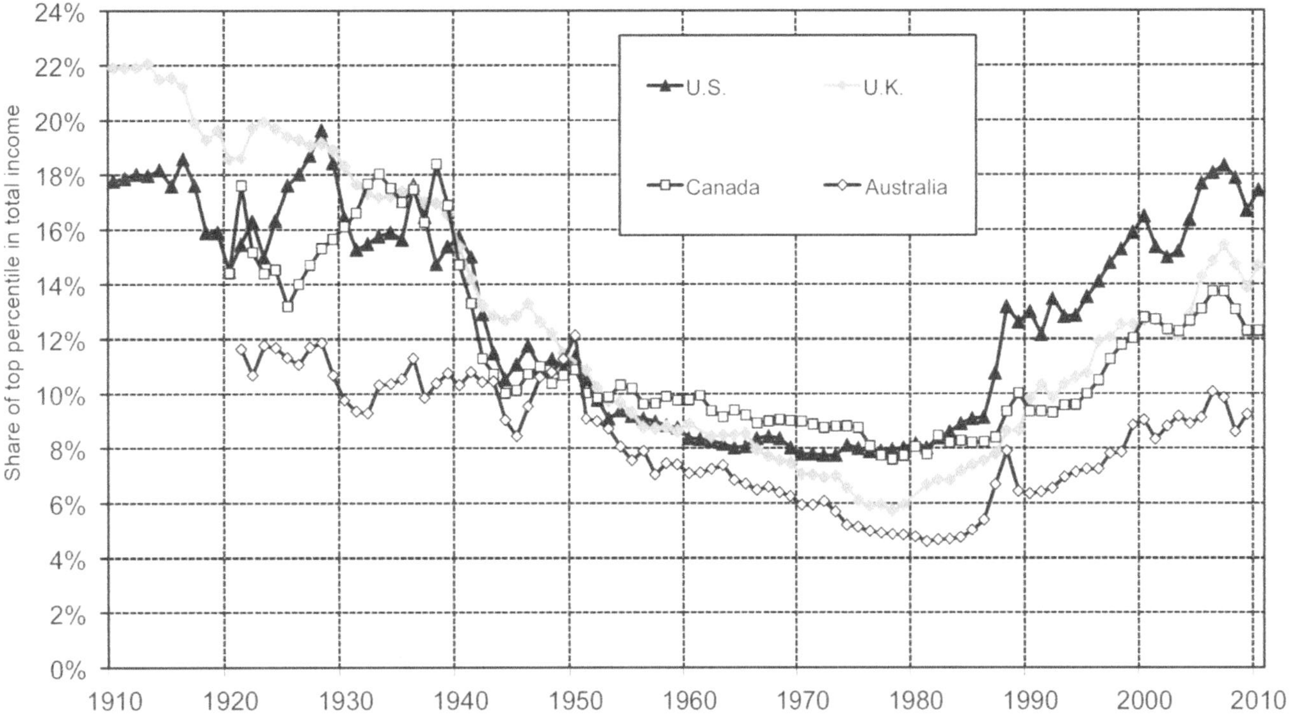

The share of top percentile in total income rose since the 1970s in all Anglo-saxon countries, but with different magnitudes. Sources and series: see piketty.pse.ens.fr/capital21c.

Figure 9.3. Income inequality: Continental Europe and Japan, 1910-2010

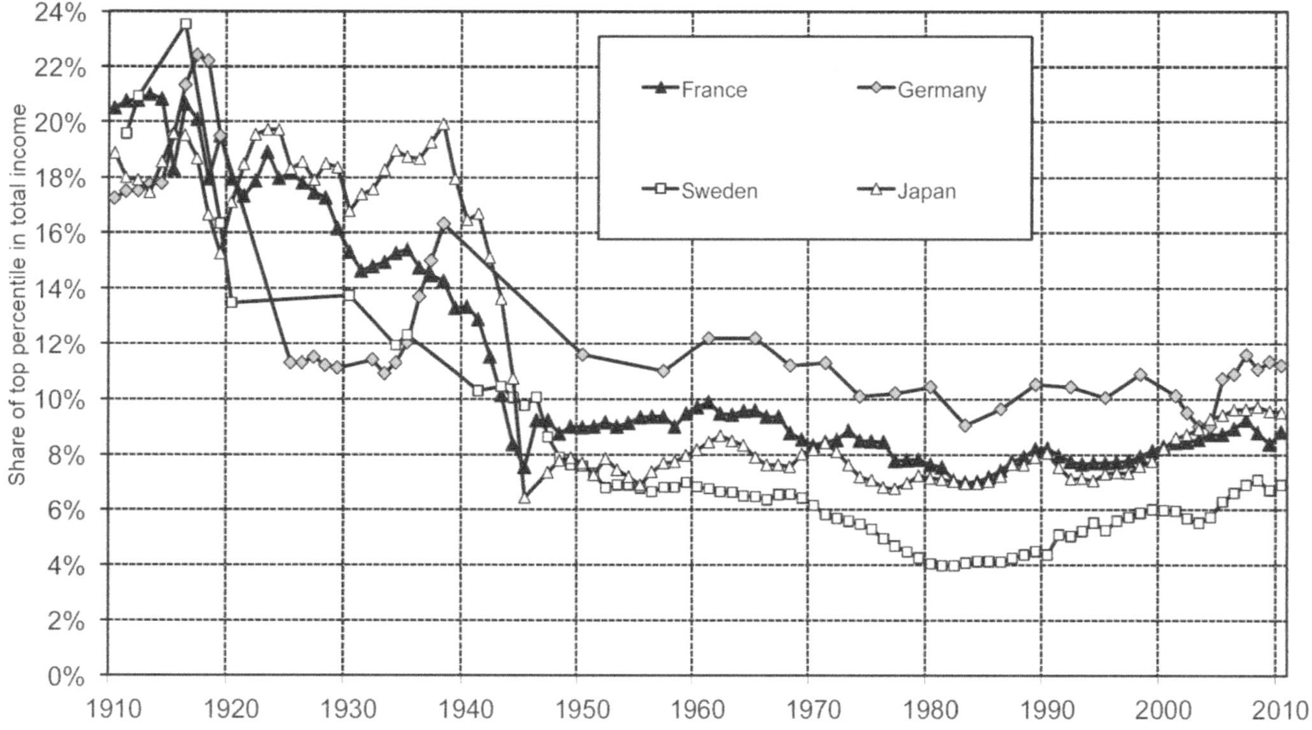

As compared to Anglo-saxon countries, the share of top percentile barely increased since the 1970s in Continental Europe and Japan. Sources and series: see piketty.pse.ens.fr/capital21c.

Figure 9.9. Income inequality in emerging countries, 1910-2010

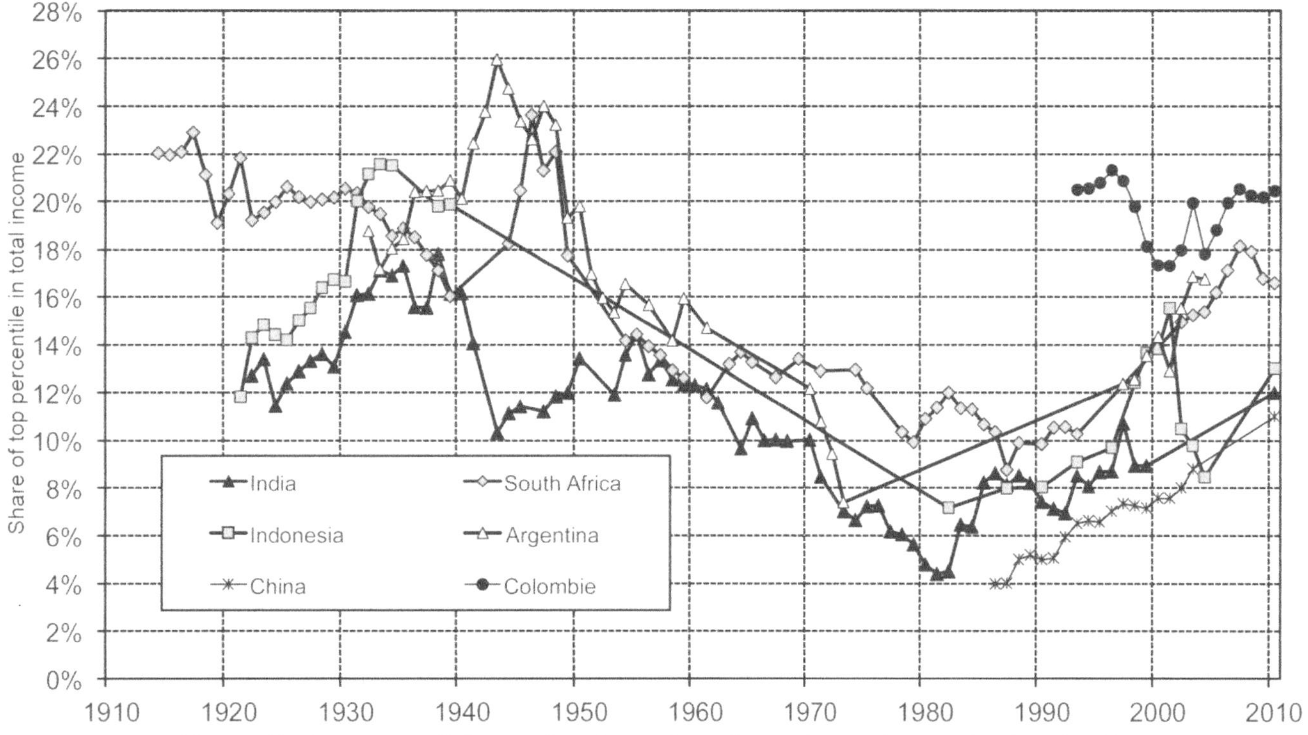

Measured by the top percentile income share, income inequality rose in emerging countries since the 1980s, but ranks below U.S. level in 2000-2010. Sources and series: see piketty.pse.ens.fr/capital21c.

with annual data points, as well as those for the Anglo-Saxon and continental Europe and Japan, for the top decile for comparison with France and the United States, but they are not presented in the book.

Piketty does present one graph for the top decile for some European countries but presents the data using only decennial averages, a highly unsatisfactory approach given the detailed data at his disposal. His intention in doing so is to focus on long term trends, but a more satisfactory approach would be to present annual values based on a 10 year moving average. Such a graph would provide more insight to how the trend is developing. Piketty's decennial average curves for Britain, France, Germany, Sweden and the United States from 1900 to 2010 is Figure 9.7. It confirms what the more detailed plots have shown: (a) at the beginning of the twentieth century, the United States was more egalitarian than the European countries; (b) the top decile's share of income decreased in all of these countries due to the shocks of 1914-1945; (c) between 1950 and 1970, the top decile's share of income was relatively stable and similar; and (d) thereafter there is significant divergence with the United States and Britain becoming much more inegalitarian with Sweden being the most egalitarian. The shocks of the World Wars had a larger impact on the European countries (and Japan) than on the United States. Piketty attributes this to the much larger shocks to capital experienced by Europe and Japan.

Figure 9.7. The top decile income share: Europe and the U.S., 1900-2010

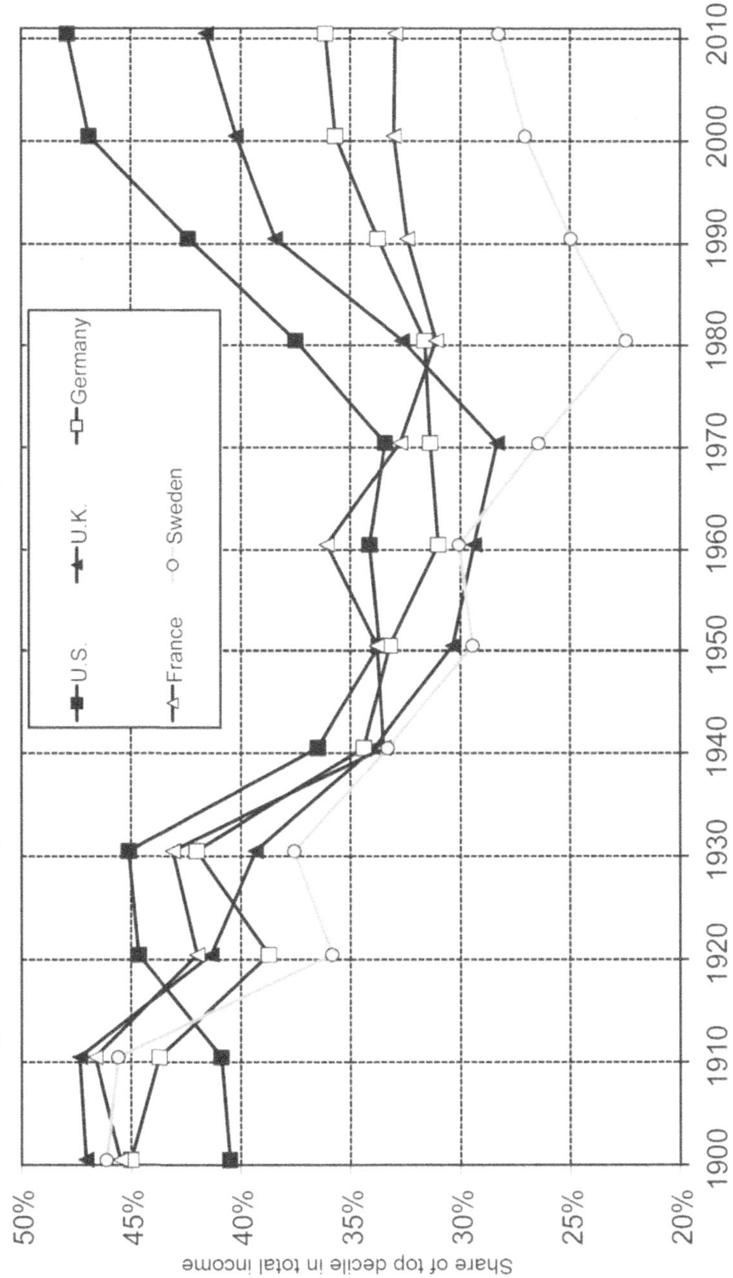

In the 1950s-1970s, the top decile income share was about 30-35% of total income in Europe as in the U.S.

Sources and series: see piketty.pse.ens.fr/capital21c.

One of the disappointments in Piketty's presentation of material on income inequality is that while he highlights the growing share of income being received by the top decile, he does not discuss or present any information about what segment of the other 90 percent is receiving a smaller share. There is no reason to expect it to be equally distributed across the entire 90 percent.

Growing Inequality in the Distribution of the Ownership of Capital

The next subject is the distribution of capital. Piketty's Figure 10.6 summarizes his results. The shares of total capital or wealth owned by the top decile and the top centile for Europe and the United States are shown in this figure. Before the figure is analyzed, a few words about its construction need to be said. The Europe curves are averages calculated from the results for three countries: Britain, France and Sweden. The individual country curves are presented in the book, and each country exhibits a pattern quite similar to the one seen in Figure 10.6. In addition, notice that for the period prior to 1910 there are only two data points, one for 1810 and one for 1870. These two values are not based on data meeting the quality of the data for the period after 1910. As such they should not be given the same credence as the more recent information.

Figure 10.6. Wealth inequality: Europe and the U.S., 1810-2010

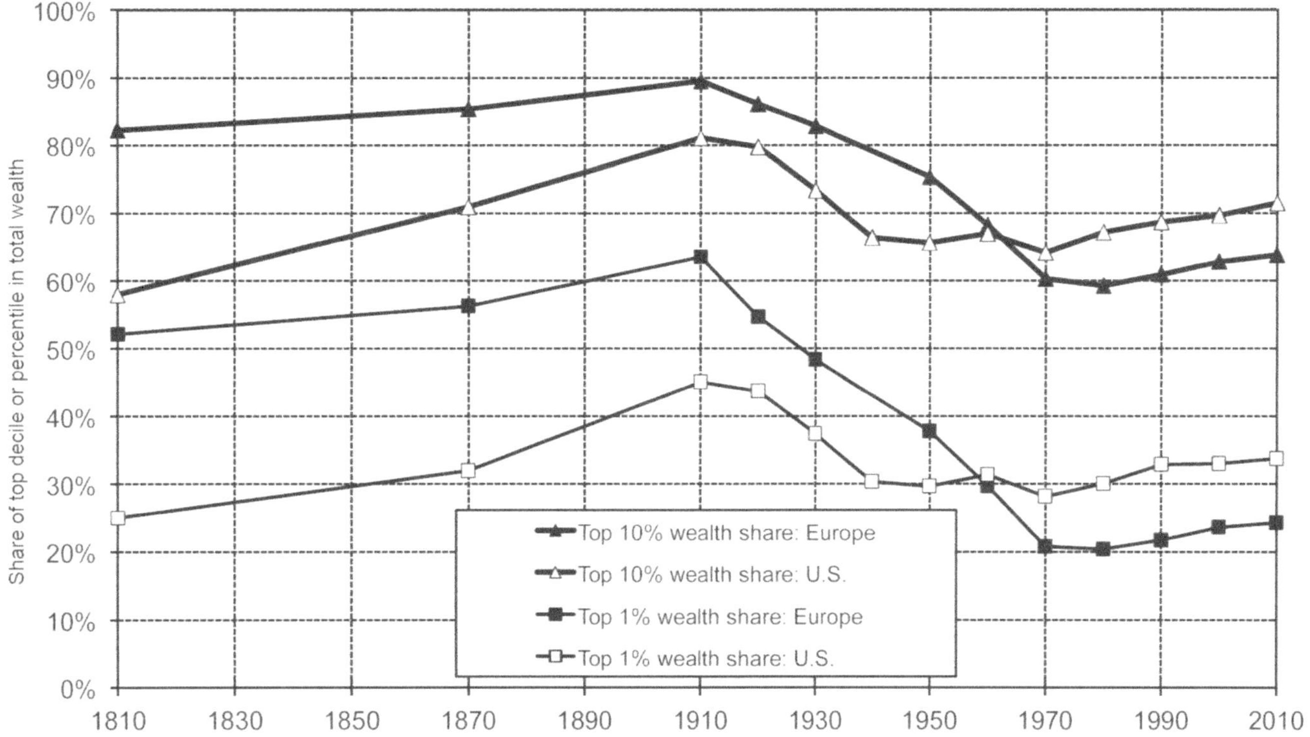

Until the mid 20th century, wealth inequality was higher in Europe than in the United States.
Sources and series: see piketty.pse.ens.fr/capital21c.

The other feature of Figure 10.6 to be aware of is that this figure shows the share of wealth owned by the top decile and the top centile of the wealth distribution. These deciles and centiles are not the same people who make up the top deciles and centiles of the income distribution discussed above. As a result, they are not directly comparable.

Piketty is fond of contrasting Europe and the United States at the beginning of the nineteenth century by pointing out that at that time Europe had more wealth inequality than the United States and that at the beginning of the twenty-first century the inequality in Europe was lower than in 1810 while it was higher in the United States. This comparison is suspect because of the poorer quality of data for the nineteenth century and because the United States was an agrarian society in the early nineteenth century playing catch up with the more advance economy of Europe. A better comparison is from the beginning of the twentieth century to today.

Focusing on the period from 1910 to 2010 in Figure 10.6 results in several conclusions. First, in both Europe and the United States there was very high inequality in the distribution of wealth. In 1910, the top decile in Europe owned 90 percent of the capital and the top decile in the United States owned 80 percent. For the top centile, the percentages were about 62 in Europe and 45 in the United States. In both cases the United States was less unequal in the distribution of capital than Europe was in 1910.

Europe and the United States both exhibited a decline in inequality of capital ownership from 1910. In the case of Europe, the top decile's share of capital declined from 90 percent to 60 percent in 1970. For the United States, its top decile's share of capital declined from 80 percent to 65 percent in 1940. The declines for the centiles are: from 62 percent to 20 percent in 1970 for Europe and from 45 percent to 30 percent in 1930 in the United States. Inequality declined faster in the United States than in Europe, but the decline went farther in Europe.

After arriving at the lowest shares of capital owned by the top deciles and centiles, the shares began to increase slowly starting in 1970. The top decile's share of capital rose from 60 percent to about 63 percent in Europe between 1970 and 2010 and from 65 percent to about 71 percent in the United States between 1970 and 2010. The top centile's share of capital increased from 20 percent to about 23 percent in Europe between 1970 and 2010 and from slightly below 30 percent to about 32 percent in the United States between 1970 and 1980.

The most striking difference between 1910 and now is the evolution of a middle class that owns between 30 and 40 percent of capital. This change in the structure of inequality in the ownership of capital is likely to continue into the twenty-first century. As a result, a significant amount of the returns to the owners of capital are not going to go to the wealthiest 10 percent.

Why is Piketty so concerned with the inequality in the ownership of capital? "The question is important, all the more, because the reduction of this type of inequality, and the income derived from it, was the only reason why total income inequality diminished during the first half of the twentieth century. As noted, inequality of income from labor did not decrease in a structural sense between 1900-1910 and 1950-1960 in either France or the United States ..., and the sharp drop in total income inequality was due essentially to the collapse of high incomes from capital." (Piketty. Page 336.) This statement goes too far; it overstates the contribution of income from capital to the sharp decline. Piketty points to France and the United states to support his claim.

An examination of Figure 8.1 for France shows that the story is more nuanced. In France, the top decile's share of total income started at around 46 percent in 1910, dropped to as low as 39 percent around 1920, grew again to as high as 46 percent around 1936, and then dropped to around 29 percent in 1945 rising to around 33 percent in the late 1940s. The top decile's share of wages started at about 26 percent in 1910, dropped to about 21 percent in 1920, grew to about 28 percent in 1933, dropped again to about 22 percent in 1943 rising to around 26 percent in the late 1940s. The ups and downs in the shares of total income and in wages mirror each other, but the size of the movements is different. The implication (because the members of the two deciles are not the same) is that between 1910 and 1945 the top decile's decline in the share of total income was 17 percentage points and the top decile's share of wages declined by 4 percentage points. This implies that perhaps a little under a quarter of the drop in total income could be due to wages. If you compare highest peak to lowest trough, wages appear to account for 41 percent of the drop in total income. Piketty gets to the result of no contribution from wages by comparing 1910 to 1950. The essence is that the contribution of the loss of capital was very large, but probably not the sole contributor. In addition, there are new labor market elements today, especially the supermanagers.

A similar analysis of Figure 8.7 for the United States implies that wages accounted for one-third of the drop in total income between 1910 and 1945. Even more informative is that when 1910 and 1950 are compared for the United States wages also impliedly account for one-third of the drop in total income. That was the comparison in France that supported Piketty's claim that labor played no role in the collapse of total income and that loss of capital was largely responsible.

<u>Return on Capital Greater than the Rate of Growth</u>

Piketty sees a future that involves the role of capital returning to the role it played before World War I. He sees capital in the future increasingly concentrated in a small share of the population, the top decile and the top centile. He offers an explanation for the pre-World War I concentration of capital, the decline in the concentration of capital in the twentieth century and his belief in the rise in the concentration of capital in the twenty-first century. His explanation is that when the after tax return on capital is greater than the growth rate of the economy, the concentration of capital will increase and when it is less than the growth rate, concentration of capital will decrease. This theory leads to what may be the most reproduced figure from the book; Figure 10.10. His explanation for the decline in the concentration of capital in the twentieth century is that the two world wars destroyed large amounts of capital and the very high tax rates implemented to finance these wars dispersed capital. In the twenty-first century, Piketty predicts a low growth rate so he predicts a large return to capital.

A quick look at Figure 10.10 inclines the reader to Piketty's point of view. But this is a very unusual figure. Notice that the figure covers the entire global economy and the time line runs from zero to 2100. This is a strange time line for a book based on thorough data analysis because there is little reliable information for the rate of return or growth rates plotted in figure 10.10 outside of the period of 1820-2010 and then the data is limited to a few countries, England and France. There is so little data underlying this figure that little credence should be given to it. The portion of Figure 10.10 on the right side covering the period from 2010 to 2100 is entirely made up of assumptions. In particular, Piketty assumes that "fiscal competition will gradually lead to total disappearance of taxes on capital in the twenty-first century; the average tax rate on capital is set at 30 percent for 1913-2012, 10 percent for 2012-2050 and 0 percent in 2050-2100". (Piketty, page 355.) Piketty assumes the global growth rate will be 3.5 percent in 2012-2030, 3.0 percent in 2030-2050, 1.7 percent in 2050-2070 and 1.4 percent in 2070-2100. (Piketty, Figure 2.5, page 101.)

Figure 10.10. After tax rate of return vs. growth rate at the world level, from Antiquity until 2100

The rate of return to capital (after tax and capital losses) fell below the growth rate during the 20th century, and may again surpass it in the 21st century. Sources and series : see piketty.pse.ens.fr/capital21c

In addition, just before Piketty presents Figure 10.10, he presents Figure 10.7 (not reproduced here) which presents actual decennial data from France on the before tax rate of return on capital and rate of growth, but for some unstated reason, the figure is limited to 1820 to 1910. Piketty uses Figure 10.7 to show that during this period the return on capital was significantly higher than the rate of growth. But this leaves the reader asking what happened in France after 1910. Figure 3 is a reconstruction of Piketty's Figure 10.7 for 1820-2010. While Figure 10.7 leaves the reader with the implication that the before tax rate of return exceeded the growth rate before but not after World War I, Figure 3, which also uses decennial data, shows that it exceeded the growth rate throughout this period up to today. (Piketty's Figure 10.7 also plots the before tax rate of return just like Figure 3.) Of course, the important series to examine is the after tax rate of return on capital.

What does the after tax rate of return on capital compared to the rate of growth look like? If Figure 3 is reproduced using decennial data with the after tax rate of return on capital in place of the before tax rate of return on capital, the after tax rate of return on capital exceeds the rate of growth for the 1820-2010 period except for a brief period around the 1960 decennial data point. These decennial based graphs can be improved upon. Piketty builds them largely from annual data series for France (especially in the twentieth century) with the objective of giving a long run perspective to the data. However, the decennial data points hide

Figure 3. Before Tax Rate of Return on Capital and Growth Rates in France: 1820-2010 (Decennial Data)

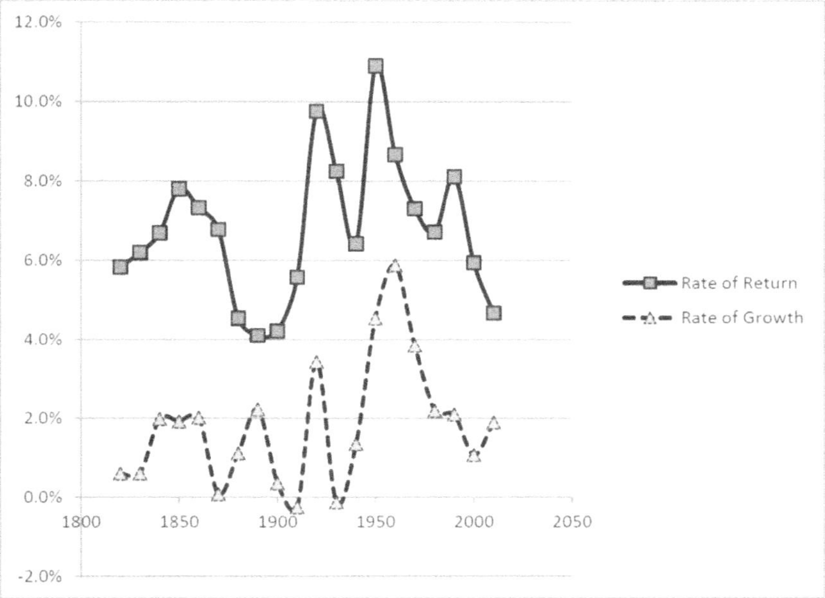

Based on data from
http://piketty.pse.ens.fr/en/capitalisback France.xls Table FR.3c and http://piketty.pse.ens.fr/capital21c Table S10.2

useful information. A preferable approach would be to construct 10 year moving averages to smooth out the short term fluctuations while providing more nuanced insight into the longer run trends. Figure 4 presents the after tax rate of return on capital and the rate of growth in France from 1897 to 2010 using 10 year moving averages. It shows that the after tax rate of return on capital was less than the rate of growth from 1945 to 1950 and from 1963 to 1969, and they were essentially equal from 1970 to 1974.

It would be interesting to examine the annual series for the United Kingdom, but the only data in Piketty's files seems to be decennial data from 1770-2010 on before tax rates of return. It implies that annual data is in a UK.xls file, but was not present in the files examined. Annual data on growth rates are available from 1855. Figure 5 is based on decennial data points. It is the British equivalent of Figure 3 for France. Again, the before tax return on capital exceeds the rate of growth throughout 1860-2010. Unfortunately, data on the after tax rate of return on capital in Britain could not be located.

The foregoing suggests that Piketty's theory about the rate of return on capital being below the rate of growth for much of the twentieth century is not supported by the available data, especially the after tax rate of return information on France. It would be desirable to have after tax return information on more countries.

Figure 4. After Tax Rate of Return on Capital and Rate of Growth in France: 1897-2010
(Annual Data; 10 Year Moving Averages)

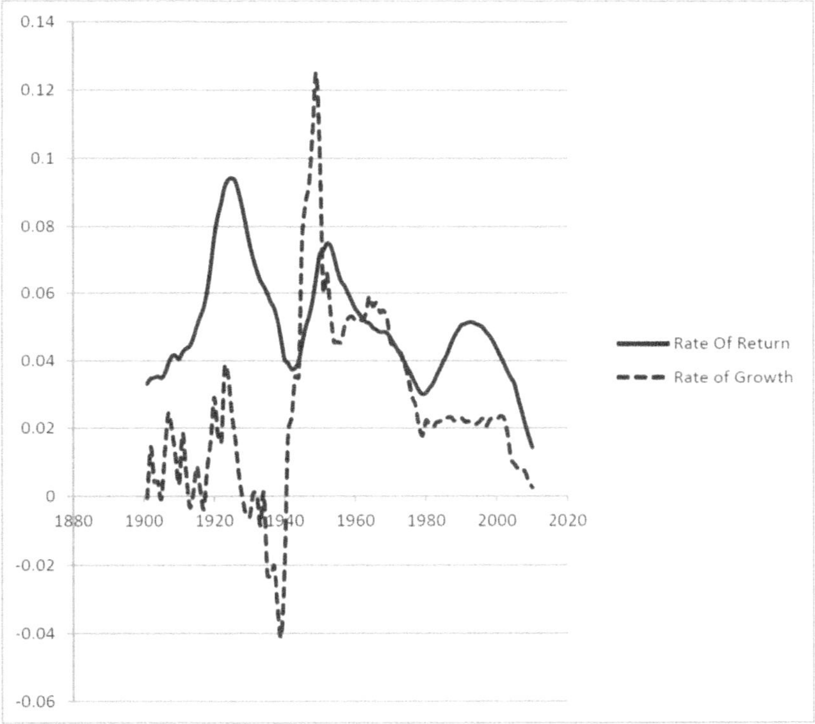

Based on data from
http://piketty.pse.ens.fr/en/capitalisback France.xls
Tables FR.3b and FR.5b

Figure 5. Before Tax rate of Return on Capital and Rate of Growth in Britain: 1860-2010 (Decennial Data)

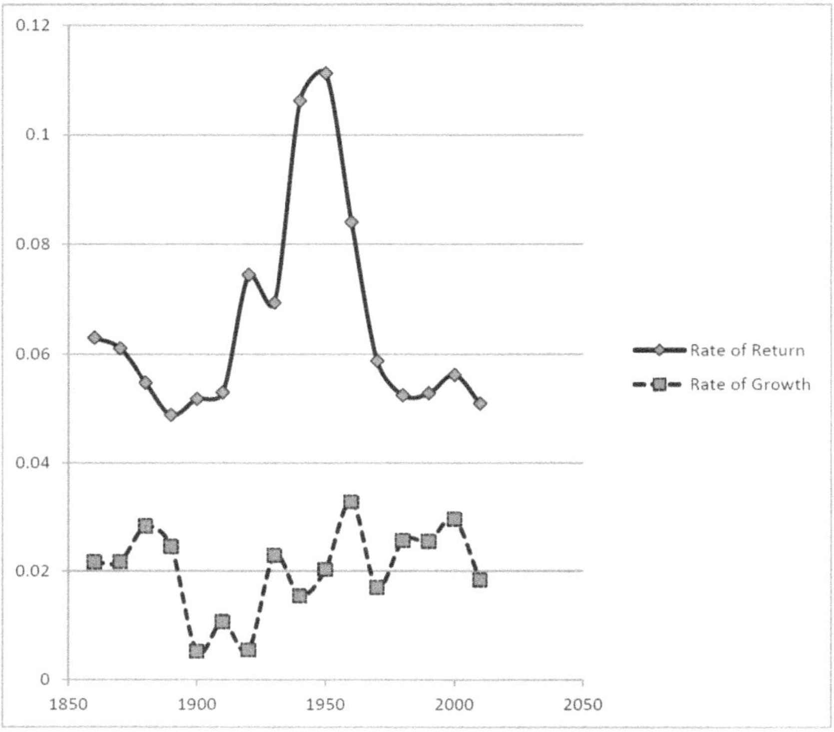

Based on

http://piketty.pse.ens.fr/capital21c Table TS6.1 and
http://piketty.pse.ens.fr/en/capitalisback UK.5b

But how does Piketty get his Figure 10.10 to show that the rate of return on capital is less than the rate of growth for the period from 1913 to 2012? There are two aspects of the rate of return on capital that Piketty raises that are not contained in Figures 3-5; one is his concern with the pure rate of return on capital and the other is capital losses. In his pure rate of return on capital, Piketty adjusts the return down to reflect the time spent by the owners of capital in managing their capital; this is above and beyond any management fees incurred from the firms employed in managing that capital. This adjustment is small, roughly 0.1 or 0.2 percentage points. Therefore, it would not alter Figures 3-5.

The other factor, capital losses, is a different story. These are the losses caused by the catastrophic events of war damage from World Wars I and II. Here, Piketty assumes an annual capital loss of 2.5 percentage points in the rate of return on capital for 1913-1950 and 0.5 percentage points for 1951-2012. There is no capital loss provision in his assumptions for the periods after 2012. Two questions present themselves with respect to this assumption. First, if these are war related capital losses, they did not occur evenly over the 37 years from 1913 to 1950, but were confined to a few years in 1914-1918 and 1941-1945. There is also the interesting feature that Piketty's Figure 4.5 shows a large loss of capital for World War I and relatively little loss in World War II for each of Britain, France and Germany as measured by the capital/income ratio. And there is the corollary issue of how do these wars support the post 1950 adjustment for capital losses.

Second, are the amounts of capital loss represented by Piketty's assumption reasonable? A large share of the decline in national capital in these three countries was the result of a steep decline in net foreign capital which declined from 176 percent of national income to 84 percent of it between 1910 and 1920 for Britain, from 123 percent to 6 percent for France in that decade and from 44 percent to 11 percent for Germany in that decade. (Piketty, pages 116, 117 and 141.) The declines in net foreign capital were not capital losses at the global level, but rather transfers from one nation to another. It is not clear how Piketty treated these in coming up with his annual capital loss figure of 2.5 percentage points for 1913-1950. However, his annual figure suggests that the loss for the 37 year period was a total of 61 percent of the initial amount. (Capital dropped to 1 minus the loss rate of 0.025, or 0.975, to the 37th power, or 39 percent of the initial amount so that 61 percent was lost.) This is close to what Britain, France and Germany experienced, but nowhere near what happened in the United States. But when net foreign capital is excluded, the loss of capital for 1913-1950 was down to 41 percent of the initial amount for Britain, 51 percent for France and 62 percent for Germany with Germany taking its largest loss in the 1920-1950 period. From a global perspective which is his purpose in Figure 10.10, Piketty's loss of capital seems too large.

Although this discussion undercuts Piketty's use of the rate of return on capital falling below the rate of growth as the explanation of the increased egalitarianism of the first half of the twentieth century, it leaves intact the argument that when the rate of return on capital is greater than the rate of growth there is opportunity for increased inegalitarianism, at least in the absence of catastrophes. Piketty's acknowledgments that catastrophe lies behind the transformation in inequality in the first half of the twentieth century is evident from the following statement. "One major lesson is already clear: it was the wars of the twentieth century that, to a large extent, wiped away the past and transformed the structure of inequality." (Piketty, page 471.) This explanation fits squarely within the analysis of the historian Walter Scheidel. In his book, *The Great Leveler: Violence and the History of Inequality from the Stone Age to the Twenty-First Century*, Scheidel identifies four great leveling forces: (a) mass mobilization warfare, (b) transformative revolution, (c) state failure and systems collapse and (d) severe epidemics. He refers to these as the Four Horsemen. Scheidel uses leveling to refer to the reduction in inequality. According to Scheidel, "history teaches us two important things about leveling. One is that radical policy interventions occur in times of crisis....The second lesson is even more straightforward: policy making can take us only so far. Time and again the compression of material imbalances within societies was driven by violent forces either that were outside human control or that are now far beyond the scope of any viable political agenda." (Scheidel, page 436.)

What does Scheidel say about his Four Horsemen? "The Four Horsemen have dismounted their steads. And nobody in his or her right mind would want them to get back on." (Scheidel, page 546.) Scheidel is not optimistic about the likelihood that traditional measures of reducing inequality such as income taxation, education and redistributive social programs can rise to the task. Part of his concern is the aging of the population, and the other is whether political majorities can be mobilized in support of such equalizing policies. He says the Four Horsemen "are gone for now. This casts serious doubt on the feasibility of future leveling." (Scheidel, page 442.) He concludes with "[a]ll of us who prize greater economic equality would do well to remember that with the rarest of exceptions, it was only ever brought forth in sorrow. Be careful what you wish for." (Scheidel, page 444.) Perhaps climate change could be the next horseman. It is more likely that climate change will make inequality worse between rich and poor nations and within nations. The poor are likely to be more exposed to the deleterious effects of climate change, more susceptible to the damage caused by climate change and less able to cope and recover from the consequences of climate change. It is possible that climate change could so worsen inequality that the four horsemen remount.

Looking forward, what are reasonable assumptions for the rate of return on capital and the rate of growth? First what are Piketty's assumptions? He assumes a rate of return on capital of 4.3 percent for 2012-2100, a tax on income from capital of 10 percent for 2012-2050 and zero percent for 2050-2100, and a rate of growth of 3.3 percent for 2012-2050 and 1.5 percent for 2050-2100. (Piketty, technical appendix excel file for Figure 10.10.) Some have expressed the view that the rate of return on capital should be higher on the basis of long run returns in the stock market. But these long run stock market returns are based on various indices which remove faltering companies before they fail and replace them with promising new companies. As a result, these stock market measures do not include the full capital losses associated with failing companies such as Bethlehem Steel, Kodak and Xerox. Hence, the measures of long run return in the stock market over estimates the rate of return on capital. Piketty's assumed rate of return on capital is not unreasonable. His assumptions about the tax on income from capital, however, strike one as too low; a tax rate in the 15-20 percent range would be more credible. His assumed tax on income from capital for 1913-2012 is 30 percent. If the tax on income from capital were 20 percent from 2012-2050, the after tax rate of return on capital would be only slightly above the rate of growth, 3.44 versus 3.3 percent. This difference would not seem to justify Piketty's fears, but the higher tax rate would not alter his concern for the 2050-2100 period.

Economists, including Piketty, treat the growth rate as the sum of the growth rate in per capita income, which is driven by productivity, and the growth rate of the population. (Technically, this is not accurate, but works as a good first order approximation.) The growth rate in world per capita income was around 1.5 percent for the 1980-2012 period and at 1.5 percent in 2016. (World Bank, 2017.) The growth rate of world population was above 1.5 percent from 1950 to around 1992 and has fallen steadily to around 1.2 percent in 2016; it is forecast to fall to 0.5 percent by 2050. (United States Census, 2017.) Based on this information, the rate of growth entering the twenty-first century was around 2.7 percent. Piketty's assumed rate of growth of 3.3 percent for

2012-2050, therefore, is not unreasonable. His assumed rate of growth of 1.5 percent for 2050-2100 is harder to evaluate, but could easily be too low.

Piketty states that the rate of "return on capital should be systematically higher than the rate of growth to be a historical fact, not a logical necessity". (Piketty, page 353.) And the data support this conclusion, but his claim that this explains the increase in equality in the first half of the twentieth century is not convincing. On reflection, Piketty's theory that the rate of return on capital being less than the rate of growth explains the reduction in capital in the first half of the twentieth century is no more than an explanation that this change was wrought by catastrophes, two world wars.

In addition, Piketty's theory about the rate of return on capital conflicts with a fundamental law of economic theory, the law of supply and demand. If capital is increasing, as Piketty claims will happen in the twenty-first century, the return to capital should decrease. A low rate of growth should also put downward pressure on the return to capital as it reduces the demand for capital.

Piketty documents the extent of inequality and its path over time with an elaborate and detailed data base, and then offers up his model of r greater than g as an explanation of growing inequality. But is the model a necessary part of his normative arguments? Piketty argues that inequality is dangerous because it fosters instability, generates unjustified differences that do not advance the common good, is increasingly easy to hide from voters thus impeding rational decision making and threatens democracy. His proposed solution is the tax on capital. These normative arguments could stand on the basis of his data analysis even if his model were incorrect.

Role of Inheritance

Even though the structure of inequality in the ownership of capital is very different today than it was 100 years ago (i.e., the capital owned by the middle class), Piketty believes that "it is all but inevitable that inheritance ... predominates over saving" in the accumulation of capital. He bases his belief on "the rate of return on capital ... [being] significantly and durably higher than the growth rate of the economy." (Piketty, pages 377-378.) A corollary of this is that, according to Piketty, "wealthier people obtain higher average returns [on capital] than less wealthy people". (Piketty, page 430.)

What evidence does Piketty present to support his belief about the growing role of inheritance? He presents Figure 11.7 which shows the share of total wealth in France that is inherited wealth for 1850 to 2010 and estimates of that share for 2010 to 2100. In 1910, inherited wealth amounted to 90 percent of total wealth. By 1970, this share dropped to about 45 percent and then climbed to about 66 percent in 2010. His projections have the share increasing to 80-90 percent by 2100. But this graph and others in the chapter focusing on inheritance are less than

Figure 11.7. The share of inherited wealth in total wealth, France 1850-2100

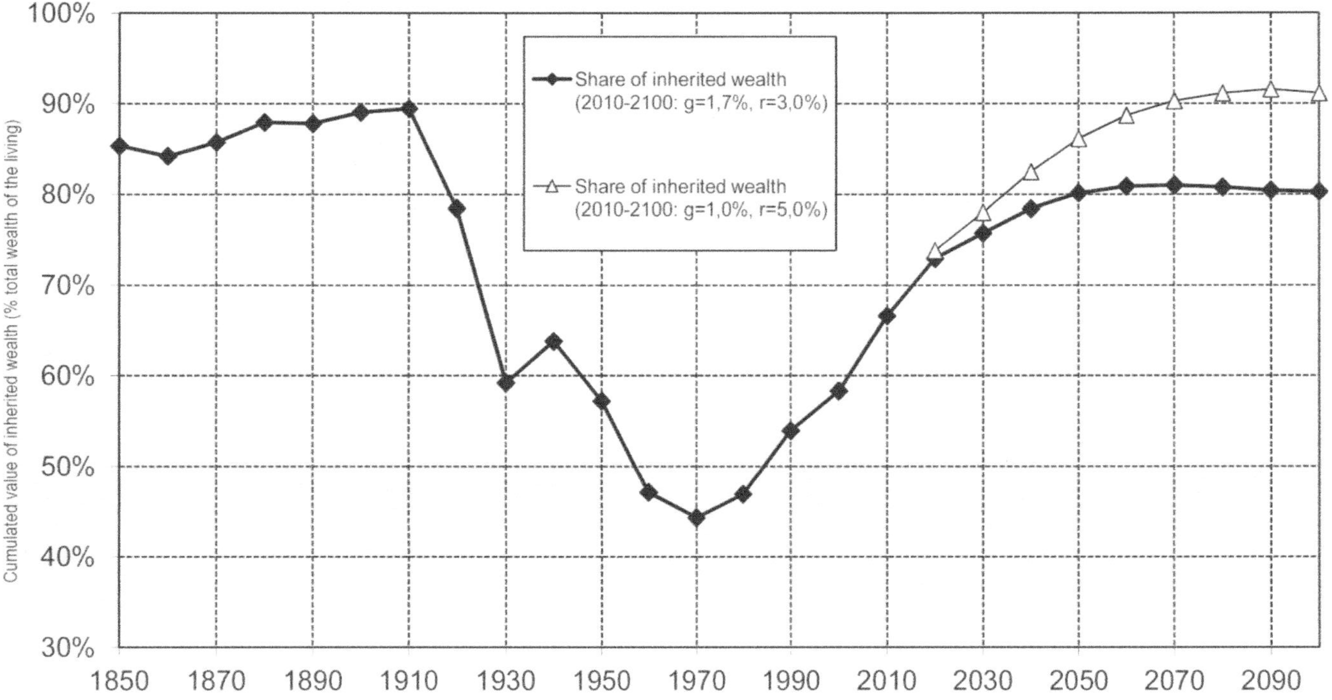

Inherited wealth represents 80-90% of total wealth in France in the 19th century; this share fell to 40%-50% during the 20th century, and might return to 80%-90% during the 21st century. Sources and series: see piketty.pse.ens.fr/capital21c

satisfactory because they do not separate the role of the wealthiest from that of the rest of the population, especially the middle class. Since the middle class gained its wealth largely between 1950 and1980, it is reasonable to expect the role of inheritance to play a larger role as the middle class pass on their accumulated wealth. Piketty acknowledges this structural difference in the inequality of the ownership of capital, but his presented evidence does not take it into account. That the inheritance of the middle class is rising does not mean that the top decile's share of wealth is rising.

Piketty's Fear and His Solution

Piketty sees an increasing concentration of capital among the wealthiest and the income from that capital systematically adding to that concentration through inherited wealth faster than capital accumulation through savings from incomes from labor, which are more broadly distributed, can keep up with. Piketty believes that "a return to the extreme concentration of wealth as in the Belle Epoque" (1871-1914) "would lead to significant political upheaval". Piketty, page 422.) He views the rate of return on capital greater than the rate of growth as a "principal destabilizing force". He views this force as "potentially threatening to democratic societies and to the values of social justice on which they are based." (Piketty, page 571.)

Piketty reviews the policies of the 1930-1960 period that contributed to a more egalitarian western society. He refers to these as the development of the "social state" and points to the increase in total tax revenues as the most direct evidence of this transformation. His data show that for Britain, France, Sweden and the United States, total tax revenues amounted to around 10 percent of national income in each country from 1870 to 1910 and that this increased substantially by 1970. In Britain, it rose to around to 40 percent of national income during the 1970-2010 period. (Piketty, page 475.) In France, it rose 40 percent by 1940 and grew to 50 percent of national income by 2010. In Sweden, it rose to 48 percent by 1970 and grew to 55 percent of national income by 2010. In the United States, it rose to around 30 percent of national income during 1970-2010. Progressive income taxation was "a crucial component of the social state". (Piketty. Page 497.) By the social state, Piketty means the increased role of government in health, education and retirement. Of course, there are other elements that could be included such as housing.

Piketty is pessimistic that the sorts of policies behind the social state can manage the growing inequality. He sees "no significant support for continuing to expand the social state at its 1930-1980 growth rates." (Piketty, page 481.) He sees progressive income taxation under threat from international tax competition and the political influence of the top income percentile. He concludes that "[w]ithout a radical shock, it seems fairly likely the current equilibrium will persist for quite some time". (Piketty, page 514.)

Piketty's solution is "a progressive annual tax on wealth – that is the net value of assets each person controls". (Piketty, page 516.) He sees this as a global tax, but entertains the idea that it could be implemented for the European Union. His proposed rates are roughly: zero percent for the first million; one percent for 1-5 million; and two percent for over 5 million. (Piketty, page 517.). In Piketty's mind "the primary purpose of the capital tax is not to finance the social state but to regulate capitalism. The goal is to first stop the indefinite increase of inequality of wealth". (Piketty, page 518.) This is reiterated by him when he writes "a capital tax is the most appropriate response to the inequality ...[rate of return on capital greater than rate of growth] as well as to the inequality of returns to capital as a function of the size of the initial stake." (Piketty, page 532.) Clearly, the annual tax on capital is designed to lower the after tax return on capital and, thereby, to impede capital accumulation by the richest.

Although Piketty describes his annual tax on capital as "utopian", he fails to apply his analysis of the unlikelihood of further success for the policies of the twentieth century to his own proposal. It is unclear why his tax proposal would not face as much international competition as progressive income taxation. He offers his claim that tax rates under a progressive income tax would have to be "confiscatory", but a tax that takes back capital, even a small one is likely to generate as much competition from tax havens. It is unclear why his tax proposal would be any less objected to by the top wealth percentile than the progressive income tax and that they would have any less success in opposing it. And it is unclear why his proposal would not also need a "radical shock" to go anywhere.

Reflections

Piketty's sketch of the role of capital in inequality is more complex than his proposed remedy assumes. Piketty's scenario goes something like: increasing capital/income ratios, growing share of national income going to capital, growing concentration of wealth in the hands of the richest and increasing income inequality. When one looks at the capital/income ratio, capital's share of national income, the share of capital owned by the top wealth decile and the share of total income of the top income decile country by country, it is more difficult to discern the pattern that underlies his proposed remedy. Consider France. National capital was stable at about 380 percent of national income for 1970-1990 and then rose to 500 percent of national income in 2000 and 600 percent in 2010. (Figure 4.5) Capital's share of national income in France remained stable at about 29 percent while its capital/income ratio increased. (Figure 6.8) (24 percent in Figure 6.5). And the share of capital owned by the top wealth decile was stable at about 61 percent from 1970 to 2010. (Piketty, Figure 10.1.) The share of total income of the top income decile in France rose in the 1980s but was stable at around 33 percent from 1990 to 2010. (Figure 8.1) The experience in France, which shows a large increase in capital, does not support a comparable increase in income inequality over the same period of time (1990-2010).

In Britain, national capital grew steadily over the 1950-2010 period from 240 to 520 percent of national income, capital's share of national income rose from about 20 percent in 1980 to about 28 percent in 2010, the share of capital owned by the top wealth decile declined from 78 percent in 1950 to 62 percent in 1970 and was stable at about 62 percent in the 1970-2010 period, and the top income decile's share of total income rose from 28 percent to 42 percent from 1970 to 2010. (Figures 4.5, 6.5, 10.3 and 9.7) The British case is interesting because the concentration of the ownership of capital was declining while the top income decile's share of total income was rising. Although capital increased greatly, increased income inequality did not result from increased concentration of the ownership of capital.

Japan presents another story. Its national capital was less than 580 percent of national income in the 1970-1985 period, rose to a fairly sharp peak of 800 percent of national income in 1990 and stabilized at about 600 percent of national income for 2000-2010. Japan had a relatively stable capital share of national income of about 25 percent for 1980-2010, and its top income percentile's share of total income was around 8 percent for the 1950-1990 period with a rise to near 10 percent in 2010. (Figures 5.7, 6.5 and 9.3) Piketty presents no data on the top income decile's performance or on the ownership of capital by the top wealth decile. Based on the data available on Japan, the Japanese experience provides little support for Piketty's scenario.

The case of the United States is yet again different. It experienced only a slight increase in capital from slightly under to slightly over 400 percent of national income over the 1950-2010 period, fairly stable capital share of national income rising from about 25 percent to about 28 percent, relatively stable concentration in the ownership of capital with the top wealth decile's share rising from 68 to 71 percent over 1970-2010, and a large increase in the top income decile's share of total income with it rising from about 34 percent in 1970 to about 47 percent in 2010. (Figures 4.8, 6.5, 10.6 and 9.7) Here, there is little change in capital and a very large increase in income inequality.

These country by country sketches throw doubt on the scenario that Piketty prefers. But isn't inequality in income distribution the concept we are interested in? And shouldn't this be examined by looking at incomes after taxes and transfer payments and taking into account non-cash benefits such as employer paid health care insurance (at least the part paid by the employer)? Piketty uses income before taxes and transfer payments and takes no account of non-cash benefits. Even with Piketty's definition of income some countries show little or approximately no increase in inequality when looking at the top decile's share of income. For example, since 1970 in France the top decile's share of income was 33.1 percent in 1970 and was 33.0 percent in 2010; in between it dropped to 29.9 percent in 1982. France's experience with its top percentile is similar. When compared to the United States, Denmark, France, Germany, Italy, Japan, Spain and Sweden have relatively small changes in their top percentile's share of income between 1970 and 2010. (Piketty,

Figures 9.3 and 9.4, pages317-318) On the other hand, Australia, Britain, Canada and the United states have experience substantial increases in income inequality since 1970. These increases are a serious concern.

What would the income distributions look like if they were calculated on income after taxes and transfer payments and taking into account non-cash benefits? It is possible to look at the distribution of disposable income (income after taxes and transfer payments) from survey data. This shows that countries can significantly reduce inequality through taxes and redistribution payments. Branko Milanovic has made these calculations for several countries, and the results clearly show that some countries make substantial reductions in inequality. (Milanovic, 2016, pages 219-220) Canada, Denmark, Finland, France, Germany, Norway, and Sweden are among those using redistribution to reduce inequality meaningfully. Britain, Israel and the United States are among those that are not. These results suggest that current tax and transfer policies can substantially reduce income inequality. The question is do we have the will to use them.

In the United States as of December 2019, two candidates for the 2020 Democratic Party nomination for President have put forth proposals for wealth tax along the lines proposed by Piketty. Senator Elizabeth Warren has proposed that households "pay an annual 2% tax on every dollar of net worth above $50 million [up to $1 billion] and a 3% tax on every dollar of net worth above $1 billion." (Warren) Senator Bernie Sanders followed with his own proposal for a graduated tax on net worth.

Senator Sanders' wealth tax starts with "a 1 percent tax on net worth above $32 million for a married couple…[and the} tax rate would increase to 2 percent of net worth $50 to $250 million, 3 percent from $250 to $500 million, 4 percent from $500 million to $1 billion, 5 percent from $1 to $2.5 billion, 6 percent from $2.5 to $5 billion, 7 percent from $5 to $10 billion, and 8 percent on wealth over $10 billion. These brackets are halved for singles." (Sanders) Both of these proposals are aimed at a wealth tax on the richest 0.1 percent of Americans, estimated as roughly 75,000 households under the Warren proposal and 180,000 households under the Sanders proposal. According to the United States Census Bureau, there were 127,586,000 households in the United States in 2018.

Globalization is a major factor in the changes in the income distribution in Britain and the United States. Milanovic has also examined this in a fascinating analysis. Again, using disposable income, he graphs the percentage increase in income for various income groups against the original income for the entire globe. This shows that the winners are those in the middle of the global income distribution, an emerging group with growing incomes largely located in China and India, and those at the top of the global income distribution, the top percentile in the rich countries. The losers are near the upper end of the global income distribution and at the bottom fifty percent of the income distributions in rich countries. (Milanovic, 2016, pages 10-11, 18-22.). This is like a hallowing out of the lower middle class in rich countries. Will this continue as globalization and technological innovation continue? How can the gains made in the rich countries be sustained while raising the incomes in the rest of the world?

Appendix

An Examination of Piketty's Second Fundamental Law of Capitalism

Thomas Piketty sets forth what he calls the Second Fundamental Law of Capitalism in his book *Capital in the Twenty-First Century.* He states that "[i]n the long run, the capital/income ratio β is related in a simple and transparent way to the savings rate s and the growth rate g according to the following formula: β=s/g". (Piketty, page 166.) We begin our investigation with the relationship between capital or wealth (used interchangeably by Piketty) and savings over time and deriving the relationship that leads Piketty to his second fundamental law. This part is just following along with Piketty's own derivation in his technical appendix. Before getting into Piketty's long run implications of the resulting equation, we study the implications of the relationship. The implications of the relationship turn out to be quite clear and testable, but Piketty never discusses them or tests them. In fact, what piqued my interest in this second law was the paucity of data on the second law, strange in a book whose hallmark is extensive data analysis. Then we examine Piketty's claim about the long run implications of the derived formula which leads him to his second law.

Piketty uses his second fundamental law to forecast the future values of the capital/income ratio. He says that "[t}he dynamic law β = s/g also enables us to think about what level of global capital/income ratio might attain in the twenty-first century". (Piketty, page 195.)

Wealth and Savings

The analysis leading Piketty to his second law starts with looking at the relationship of wealth and savings over time. The national wealth at time t+1 is equal to the national wealth at time t plus the net national savings during time t. In equation form, this is

$$W_{t+1} = W_t + S_t$$

where W refers to national wealth and S refers to net national savings. If we let Y refer to national income and divide the preceding equation by Y_{t+1}, we get the following

$$\frac{W_{t+1}}{Y_{t+1}} = \frac{W_t}{Y_{t+1}} + \frac{S_t}{Y_{t+1}}$$

Next, we use the relationship between the two Ys to modify the equation. Note that $Y_{t+1} = (1+g_t)Y_t$ where g_t is the growth rate of national income in year t. With this substitution, the equation becomes

$$\frac{W_{t+1}}{Y_{t+1}} = \frac{W_t}{(1+g_t)Y_t} + \frac{S_t}{(1+g_t)Y_t}$$

Notice that the W/Ys are by definition Piketty's national capital/income ratios. Using this information transforms the equation to

$$\beta_{t+1} = \frac{\beta_t}{1+g_t} + \frac{S_t}{(1+g_t)Y_t}$$

Now, note that S/Y is the net national savings rate s. Making this substitution leads to

$$\beta_{t+1} = \frac{\beta_t}{1+g_t} + \frac{s_t}{1+g_t} = \frac{\beta_t + s_t}{1+g_t} = \beta_t \left(\frac{1+\left(\frac{s_t}{\beta_t}\right)}{1+g_t} \right)$$

Unlike Piketty, we pause here to examine this relationship more closely by asking what it says. It relates events in time t+1 to events in time t. It has three specific things to say about this relationship, and they all relate to the value of s_t relative to the value of the product of β_t and g_t. These are as follows:

1. When $1 + \left(\frac{s_t}{\beta_t}\right) > 1 + g_t$, $\beta_{t+1} > \beta_t$. This is the same condition as $s_t > \beta_t g_t$.
2. When $1 + \left(\frac{s_t}{\beta_t}\right) = 1 + g_t$, $\beta_{t+1} = \beta_t$. This is the same condition as $s_t = \beta_t g_t$.
3. When $1 + \left(\frac{s_t}{\beta_t}\right) < 1 + g_t$, $\beta_{t+1} < \beta_t$. This is the same condition as $s_t < \beta_t g_t$.

This means that $\beta_{t+1} - \beta_t$ is positive, zero or negative when $s_t - \beta_t g_t$ is positive, zero or negative, respectively.

This is a relationship that Piketty's data should allow us to examine. Note that nothing suggests that β is converging to any value, more on this later. Piketty's data for the United States can be found at gabriel-zucman.eu/files/PSZ2016DataAppendix.pdf. The capital/income ratio, national net savings rate and growth rate are found in Table US.5b. This table covers 1870 to 2010. However, yearly observations of the capital/income ratio are only available for 1916-2010. The first thing to look at is the correlation coefficient between $\beta_{t+1} - \beta_t$ and $s_t - \beta_t g_t$. For the period 1872-2010, the correlation coefficient is 0.21. (Missing data in 1870 for one variable and lagged relationship accounts for the 1872 start). Limiting the period of analysis to the years with individual observations, namely 1917-2010, produces a correlation coefficient of 0.37.

The next step is to graph the two terms over the 1917-2012 period. The results are shown in Figure A-1. They are quite striking in that the two terms move fairly closely in parallel for the period except for the years 1995-2010. If the correlation coefficient is calculated for the period 1917-1994, it rises to 0.42. What has happened in the 1995-2010 period? Or is there some inconsistency in the way the data was put together?

Another reason for the deviations between these two terms could be the violation of Piketty's assumption that asset and consumer prices evolve on average in the same way. If they do not, capital gains and losses need to be taken into account. Then the basic formula for change in national wealth becomes

$$W_{t+1} = W_t + S_t + KG_t$$

where KG_t is the capital gain or loss during period t.

Figure A-1. Change in National Capital/Income Ratio ($\beta_t - \beta_{t-1}$) Compared With Changes in $s_{t-1} - \beta_{t-1}g_{t-1}$: United States 1917-2012 (Same as Figure 1)

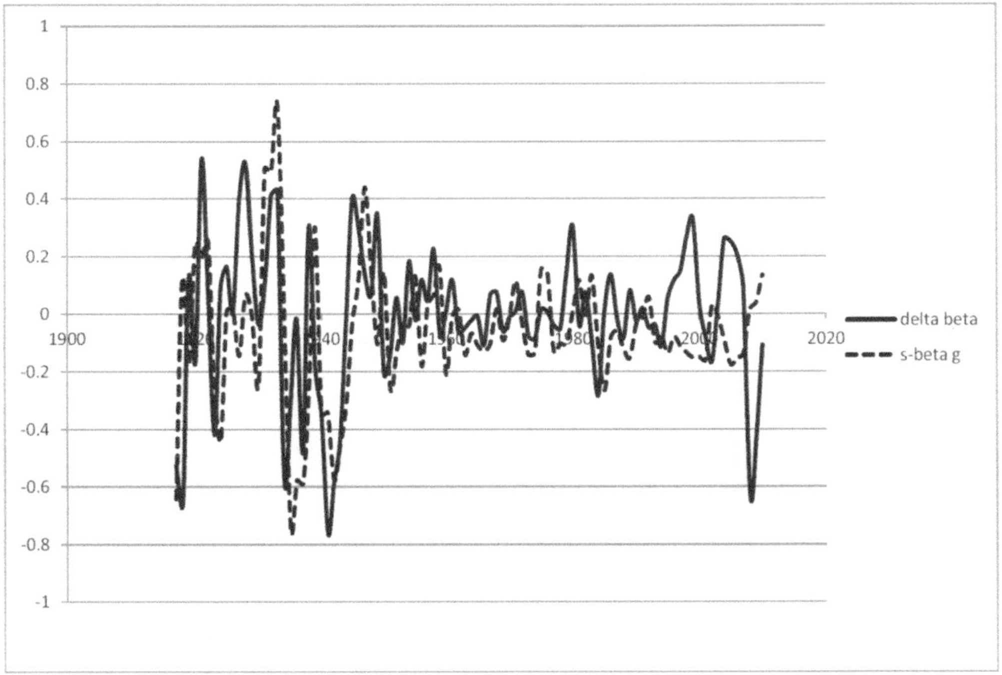

Source: Based on data in the Zucman-Piketty usa,xls file, Table US.5b

We proceed as before and divide by Y_{t+1} to get

$$\frac{W_{t+1}}{Y_{t+1}} = \frac{W_t}{Y_{t+1}} + \frac{S_t}{Y_{t+1}} + \frac{KG_t}{Y_{t+1}}$$

The first two terms on the right-hand side are the same as before leading to

$$\beta_{t+1} = \beta_t \left(\frac{1+ \left(\frac{s_t}{\beta_t}\right)}{1+g_t} \right) + \frac{KG_t}{(1+g_t)Y_t}$$

or

$$\beta_{t+1} = \beta_t \left(\frac{1+ \left(\frac{s_t}{\beta_t}\right)}{1+g_t} \right) + \frac{q_t}{(1+g_t)}$$

where $q_t = \frac{KG_t}{Y_t}$ and is real rate of capital gain or loss.

Unfortunately, there is scarce evidence on this variable except by inference. Piketty and Zucman discuss this in a 2014 paper. However, if we study Figure A- 1, we can see if the deviations are consistent with this revised formula. There are three large inconsistencies after 1995: during 1995-1999 and 2004-07, $\beta_{t+1} - \beta_t$ was larger than the other term predicted. This could be due to capital gains rising relative to consumer prices, and both periods are consistent with this, namely the run up to the dot com bust and the Great Recession. The third period was 2008-2010 when $\beta_{t+1} - \beta_t$ was smaller than the other term predicted. This could be due to capital losses relative to consumer prices which would be consistent with the Great Recession occurring at that time. That leaves the obvious question of why didn't something similar happen around the Great Depression. Although there is a slight sign of the run up effect in 1927-28, there is no similar effect to that of the Great Recession during the Great Depression.

More importantly, this alternate expression for the national capital/income ratio does not lead to Piketty's second fundamental law because in it $\beta_{t+1} \neq \beta_t$ when $s_t = \beta_t g_t$.

Everything that was presented above for the national capital/income ratio and the national net savings rate applies equally to the private capital/income ratio and private net savings rate. If the same exercise is performed with the private data, the correlation coefficients between the two terms are 0.18 for 1872-2010, 0.34 for 1917-2010 and 0.42 for 1917-1994. These are quite similar to what the comparable correlation coefficients are for the national data. The graph of these two terms is shown in Figure A- 2. It is also similar to the comparable graph for the national data.

Figure A-2. Change in Private Capital/Income Ratio ($\beta_t - \beta_{t-1}$) Compared With Changes in st-1 - βt-1gt-1 : 1917-2010

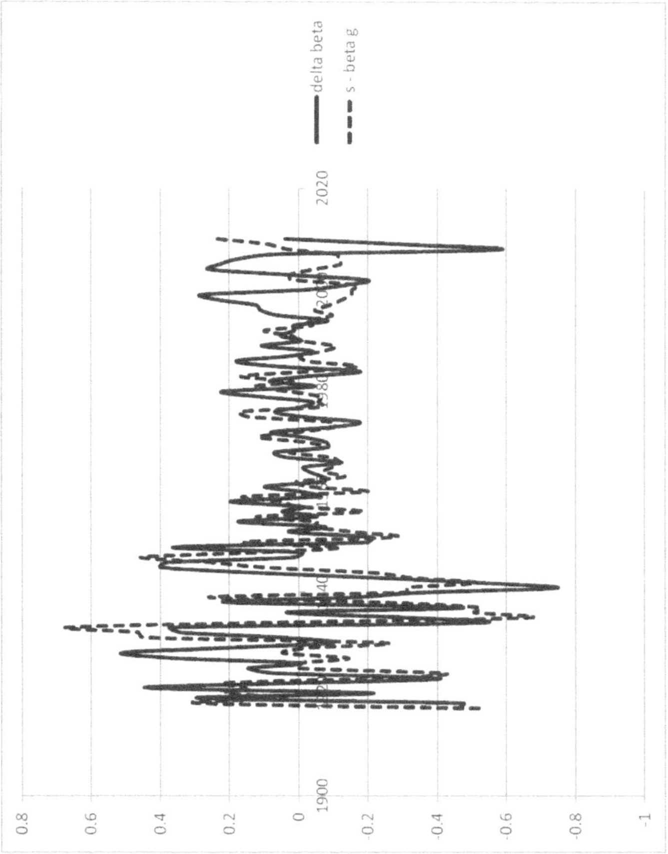

Source: Zucman-Piketty usa.xls file, Tables US.5a and US.5b.

Second Fundamental Law

To get to his second fundamental law of capitalism, Piketty asserts that in the long run the national capital/income ratio will equal the ratio of the national net savings rate to the national growth rate. It is obvious from his data that the national capital/income ratio does not equal the ratio of the national net savings rate to the national growth rate. This leads

Piketty to his claim that "this is an asymptotic law". (Piketty, page 168.) What is an asymptote? An asymptote is a line that a curve approaches as the variable approaches plus or minus infinity. The essence of an asymptote is that it is a limit on a function as the variable(s) of interest approach +/- infinity. Recall how Piketty gets to his second fundamental law; he gets it from the relationship that we have been analyzing, namely

$$\beta_{t+1} = \frac{\beta_t + s_t}{1 + g_t} = \beta_t \left(\frac{1 + \left(\frac{s_t}{\beta_t}\right)}{1 + g_t} \right)$$

Notice that if $s_t = \beta_t g_t$, $\beta_{t+1} = \beta_t$. Economists like to point to such a situation as a steady state. The problem is that there is nothing about the equation that suggests that it will inevitably approach such a steady state. As we have seen, it is just one of three possible situations that may occur in any year. If $\beta_{t+1} = \beta_t$, the relationship would have to be asymptotic. What are the variables that are to approach infinity? Are they s and g? If they were s and g, the term $= \frac{\beta_t + s_t}{1 + g_t}$ approaches 1 as s and g approach infinity. That is clearly not what Piketty has in mind; nor does it make any economic sense as s and g are relatively small numbers that are not even likely to approach one, let alone infinity. So, is it that this expression expanded to its infinite implication has an asymptote? What does that expansion look like?

$$\beta_{t+n} = \left(\frac{1+\left(\frac{s_{t+n-1}}{\beta_{t+n-1}}\right)}{1+g_{t+n-1}}\right)\left(\frac{1+\left(\frac{s_{t+n-2}}{\beta_{t+n-2}}\right)}{1+g_{t+n-2}}\right)\quad\left(\frac{1+\left(\frac{s_t}{\beta_t}\right)}{1+g_t}\right)\beta_t$$

What is the limit of this expression as n approaches infinity? It does not approach any value or relationship. It is not asymptotic.

Does Piketty's data shed any light on the issue? The only data Piketty presents on this issue is a table with the average growth and savings rates for a forty-year period (1870-2010). For the United States, the national growth rate for that period is 2.8 percent and the savings rate is 7.7 percent (Piketty, Table 5.1). The implication is that these are long run rates. If we were to have the long run value of the capital/income ratio, what would a graph of it look like relative to a plot of the annual value of the capital/income ratio? It would seem reasonable to expect the annual values to move towards the long run value of the capital/income ratio. This would seem to involve the observed capital/income ratio moving back and forth across the long run capital/income ratio.

Forty year moving averages of the national growth rate and the national savings rate can be calculated for the years 1891 to 1990. These can be viewed as estimates of the long run growth and net savings rate. And the ratio of the 40-year moving average of the national net savings rate to the 40-year moving average of the growth rate can be used as an estimate of the long run values of the capital/income ratio. These 40 year moving averages have been calculated from Piketty's data. As a check, the 40 year moving averages for 1990 should equal the values Piketty gave in his Table 5.1. The calculated 40 year moving average came out exactly the same as the number in Table 5.1, but the calculated value of the national net savings rate came out to as 5.8 percent instead of the 7.7 percent in Table 5.1. Closer study of Table 5.1 shows that Piketty reports national growth rates in it but not national net savings rates; instead he reports private net savings rates. It is not clear why he does this since logic suggests that the numerator and denominator of the capital/income ration should be calculated from the same universe. If the 40-year moving average of Piketty's private net saving rates are calculated, the number for 1990 is 8.3 percent. Searching through his data files has not cleared this up. In any case these numbers suggest long run capital/income ratios for 1990 ranging from 2.1 to 3.0.

Next, the observed capital/income ratio and the estimated long run capital income ratio are plotted for the period 1891 to 1990. The results for the national capital/income ratio are shown in Figure A- 3.

The observed capital/income ratio does not behave as if it is approaching the long run capital/income ratio. Instead it always lies above the long run capital/income ratio. In addition, in recent times the long run capital/income ratio is falling and not rising as Piketty claims. But Piketty highlighted the private savings rate in his Table 5.1. Does this mean that he is more interested in the private capital/income ratio? The results for the private capital/income ratio are shown in Figure A-4.

Figure A-3. Observed and Long Run Beta for National Capital: 1891-1990

(Same as Figure 2)

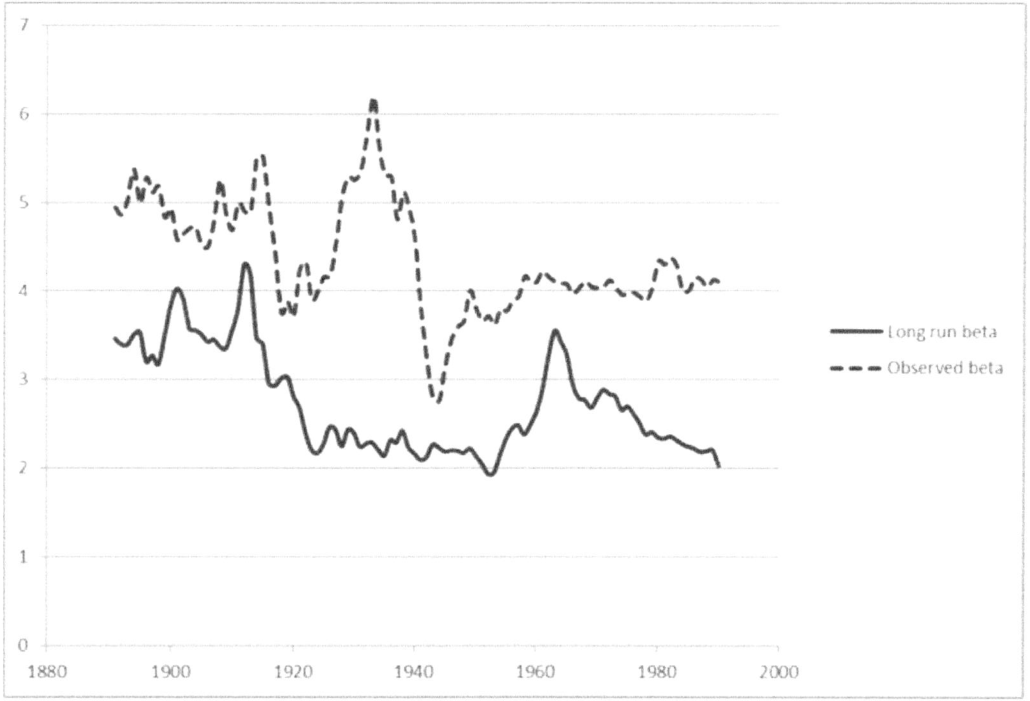

Source: Zucman-Piketty usa.xls file, Table US.5b.

Figure A-4. Observed and Long Run Beta for Private Capital: 1891-1990

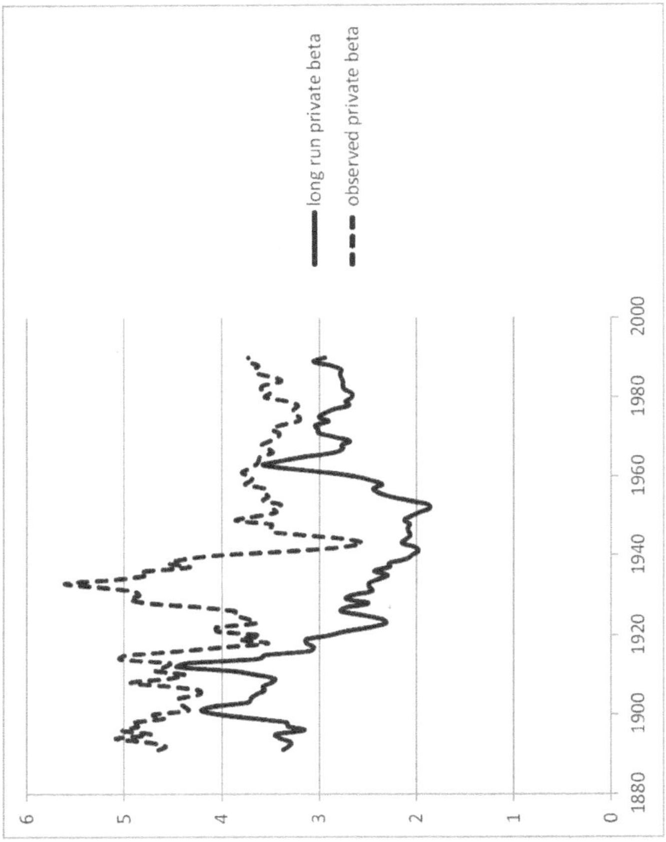

Source: Zucman-Piketty usa.xls file, Table US.5b.

The two lines are closer to one another, but they still do not display the type of behavior one would expect. One improvement is that the observed and long run private capital/income ratios are moving in the same direction during the most recent twenty years; both are increasing.

What are we to make of these results? I suppose they indicate that the second fundamental law of capitalism may not be a reliable forecasting tool for the capital/income ratio in the future.

References

Milanovic, Branko, "The Return of 'Patrimonial Capitalism': A Review of Thomas Piketty's *Capital in the Twenty-First Century*," *Journal of Economic Literature* (2014), 519-534.

Milanovic, Branko. *Global Inequality: A New Approach for the Age of Globalization* Cambridge, MA: The Belknap Press, 2016).

Piketty, Thomas, *Capital in the Twenty-First Century* (Cambridge, MA: Harvard University Press, 2014).

Piketty, Thomas, and Gabriel Zucman, "Capital is Back: Wealth-Income Ratios in Rich Countries 1700-2010," *Quarterly Journal of Economics* (2014), 1255-1310.

Sanders, Bernie, "Tax on Extreme Wealth", ttps://berniesanders.com/issues/tax-extreme-wealth/, visited on October 27, 2019.

Scheidel, Water, *The Great Leveler: Violence and the History of Inequality from the Stone Age to the Twenty-First Century* (Princeton: Princeton University Press, 2017).

United States Census Bureau, "Families and Households",Historical Household Tables, Table HH-3, https://www.census.gov/topics/families/families-and-households.html, visited on October 28, 2019.

United States Census, "World Population Growth Rates: 1950-2050", census.gov/population/international/data/idb/worldgrgraph.php accessed on June 5, 2017.

Warren, Elizabeth, "Ultra-Millionaire Tax", https://elizabethwarren.com/ultra-millionaire-tax, visited on October 27, 2019.

Weil, David, "Capital and Wealth in the Twenty-First Century," *American Economic Review* (2015), 34-37.

World Bank, "GDP per capita growth (annual) %", data.world.bank/indicator/NY.GDP.PCAP.KD.ZG accessed on June 6, 2017.

Acknowledgements

Thanks to Peter Temin for giving a course on Thomas Piketty's *Capital in the Twenty-First Century* at the Harvard Institute for Learning in Retirement that stimulated my interest in this topic and led to this manuscript. Thanks to the members of that class for the interesting discussions and exchange of ideas. Thanks to Karl Schafer for insightful comments on a draft that led to significant improvements. And, last but not least, thanks to Penny Schafer who read several drafts and contributed immensely to an improved outcome. Needless to say, responsibility for the result rests with me.

Robert Schafer

About the Author

Robert Schafer has a B.S. in physics from Union College, a M.S. in physics from Yale University, a J.D. from Harvard Law School and a Ph.D. in urban planning (with a concentration in economics) from Harvard University. He was an associate professor of City and Regional Planning at Harvard University. He is the author of *The Suburbanization of Multifamily Housing*, co-author of an early quantitative analysis of racial and gender discrimination in mortgage lending, *Discrimination in Mortgage Lending*, and a co-author of *Housing America's Elderly*. He is a co-editor of *Housing Urban America.*

Made in United States
Cleveland, OH
05 November 2026

47672908R00059